D1242426

JOY
ON COMMAND

UNLOCK
HEALTH, HOPE AND HAPPINESS
INSIDE YOUR SOUL.

O. TRAVIS MARSHALL IV

JOY ON COMMAND

*Unlock Health, Hope And Happiness
Inside Your Soul.*

O. Travis Marshall IV

This book is dedicated...

...to my talented wife, Holly, as well as my brilliant son, Trent. Thanks for standing by me in this long time dream. Thanks for believing in me and loving me.

...to my Pastors, George & Karen, who have always been a source of encouragement, allowing me the time needed to complete this book. Also to my Christian World Church family for their support. (Additional and special thanks to Pedro and Debbie, who were willing to test out this content with their groups.)

...to Steve, John, Roger, Ron and Todd. This group of classy gentlemen (all incredibly industrious themselves) kept me encouraged throughout the process. Thank you for also providing sage-like insight along the journey to this book's completion.

PRAISE FOR BOOK

Several years ago, a friend challenged me with a question. He asked, "in our attempts to follow the Great Commission, which Jesus gave to his disciples, do we even know what He specifically commanded us to obey and go teach?" Thus began a wonderful two year journey of discovery, discipleship and obedience.

Joy On Command, the content used for this journey was provided by Travis Marshall, written in a thought-provoking, highly practical and thoroughly engaging style.

His reflections on the what Christ has commanded all of us, have been transformational in my own walk. My "aha moment" along this journey - one that Travis so clearly guides us to understand - has been that obedience to Jesus' commands is far from burdensome. Obedience actually leads us to abiding and enduring joy.

I'm confident that this book will be a major blessing to the larger Christian community, and bring this same joy to countless others as well.

Rev. Dr. Roger A. Dermody
Executive Director at Friends of Forman Christian
College

I highly recommend *Joy On Command* by Travis Marshall IV. This book is a powerful and transformative guide that provides a simple and effective strategy for achieving the joy that Christ commands us to have. Travis' approach is easy to follow and has already made a significant impact on my own life.

Since reading *Joy on Command*, I have experienced a breakthrough in my ability to receive the joy promised in scripture. Travis' strategy is rooted in solid biblical principles and provides a clear roadmap to experience true joy in our lives.

One of the things I appreciate most about this book is that it is not just a theoretical guide but a practical one. Travis shares real-life examples and personal anecdotes that help bring the principles to life and make them easy to apply in our own lives.

John Cunningham
Founder of FreedomHour and Mental Health Coach

In 46 years as a follower of Jesus, I have never been blessed more than being part of the discipleship teachings of *Joy on Command*.

Pastor Travis Marshall invites us to walk closer with Jesus, through the power of the Holy Spirit, to live out the commands of Christ daily.

I encourage every Christian to read this book, and more importantly, allow it to lead you into an intimate walk with the Master.

Dr. Ron Eccles
The "Success Doctor" www.DrRonEccles.com

The responsibility of a tour guide is to introduce and explain to those on a journey the things that make the journey unique, beautiful, and framed in the context of foreign culture. The tour guide is often a traveler as well, where things previously overlooked are now shared with others and the experience for all is amplified.

Travis Marshall IV is such a tour guide for believers who have elected, along with him, to follow Jesus on a journey of discipleship and sanctification. Unlike a journey where travelers reach a destination, though, our travels are more about learning, understanding, and ultimately embracing the reality that we are being formed into messengers of God's gift to all the world, reflecting His mercy and undeserved grace. Similarly, who of us in a conversation has not asked for clarification or to have words repeated for deeper understanding?

How much more important, then, is the tour guide's responsibility to see to it that what is seen or heard is rightly understood—especially for those who want to experience the journey in full measure! Here again, Travis masterfully steps in to clarify what God declares as truth and provides perspective for the journey we all share.

I am privileged to call Travis Marshall IV a fellow traveler, a dedicated tour guide, and a good friend. I have been privileged to witness, first-hand, his journey and can say without hesitation that my journey has been enhanced by his. I highly recommend *Joy on Command* without any hesitation whatsoever.

M. Todd Petersen
President, Wholeness HQ

FOREWORD

It's my honor to write the foreword for Joy on Command, an incredible book written by my dear friend, Travis. As a pastor at Christian World Church, Travis has dedicated his life to spreading the message of the love and grace of Jesus Christ. In this book, he expertly shows us how following the commands of Christ can lead to a life of complete joy.

I have had the privilege of working alongside Travis on this project for the past two years, and I have seen firsthand the passion, dedication, and expertise he has brought to this work.

Through his years of ministry he has seen the struggles that many Christians face in their mental and emotional health. He offers both the practical and actionable steps that Jesus gave us to overcome these challenges and find true joy in our faith.

One of the things I admire most about this book (and Travis) is how it helps us see our faith in a new light. Travis encourages us to see that obeying Christ's commands is not simply a list of do's and don'ts, but rather a path to true freedom and fulfillment. He shows how the teachings of Christ, when understood and applied correctly, can bring about profound changes in our thoughts, emotions, and behaviors. Thus helping us experience a deeper level of joy and peace in our lives.

He explains that joy is not something that can be manufactured or forced, but rather, it is a byproduct of living in obedience to Jesus' commands. He shows us that when we do, we are living in alignment with our true purpose and design, and it is this alignment that leads to a deep sense of fulfillment.

This book also addresses the common misconceptions and pitfalls that can get in the way of experiencing true joy in our faith, providing useful insights and tools to help us overcome these obstacles and find true joy in our faith.

I believe that *Joy On Command* will become a valuable resource for anyone looking to deepen their understanding of their faith and wanting to find greater happiness in their lives. It is my hope that this book will help transform the lives of many Christians and bring them closer to the love and grace of Jesus Christ.

Joy On Command is a guide, a companion, and a friend that will walk with readers as they discover the joy that comes from living in obedience to God's commands. Best of all, it is written in a way that is easy to understand, relatable, practical and most importantly... actionable.

I believe that this book will have a lasting impact on the lives of those who read it. I am honored to have been a part of this project and I am excited for the world to read and benefit from the wisdom and insights contained within these pages.

Steve Cunningham, Founder and CEO
Readitfor.me, Growitfor.me, Getwetree.com,
CompleteJoy.io

CONTENTS

HOW TO ENJOY THIS BOOK

*...let God transform you **into a new person by
changing the way you think. Then you will learn
to** know God's will for you, **which is** good **and**
pleasing **and** perfect.*

Romans 12:2 NLT

A **GOOD** way to enjoy this book is to simply read it straight through and pull from the main ideas in each chapter.

An even **BETTER** way would be to read a chapter at a time. Then answer these three statements waiting for you at the end of each chapter:

1. My TAKE AWAY from this chapter is...

2. This chapter makes me GRATEFUL because...

3. I will TAKE ACTION for this by...

Pro Tip for #3: Be creative. Make it as simple and doable as you can. Something that can be done within the next twenty-four hours. Even if it feels silly or insignificant, you'll be amazed at how Scripture takes on a new and exhilarating expression as you attempt to live them out. Some of these you'll enjoy doing so much that you'll want to make a new habit out of it.

The **BEST** way to enjoy this book would be to do the *BETTER* way (described above) AND THEN ALSO challenge your small group, family, friends, co-workers or classmates to join along in this epic journey with you!

And Coming Soon...

The absolute *HABU* ("highest and best use") would be to pair this book along with our soon to be released CompleteJoy NanoCourse. Here you will experience an even deeper dive into proven mental health exercises that pair perfectly (and that yield powerful results) with each individual command outlined in this book. Both these resources together serve as a one-two punch. An integrated combo that is sure to rocket you along toward a better grasp of how to bring your thought life into alignment with God's Word.

If interested in learning more about this companion resource, make sure to connect with me directly. (My social media handles are in the back of this book under the "Connect With The Author" section.)

JOY STARTS HERE!!!

If you keep My commandments, you will remain in My love; just as I have kept My Father's commandments and remain in His love.

These things I have spoken to you so that My joy may be in you, and that your joy may be made full.

John 15:10-11 NASB

Joy: Real and reachable. Authentic and abundant.

Is there really such a thing? Isn't joy merely some abstract, subjective state of mind?

The foundation for this entire book can be found in John 15:10-11. (Mentioned above.) When you obey Christ's commands, He commands His joy in your life! Jesus reveals His master key, unlocking the joy-filled life that you were designed to live. Maybe you just needed to hear that first:

You are capable of experiencing complete joy.

This can be true no matter what season of life this book finds you, but it will take both your belief and even more decisively, your action.

To be sure, this journey you're about to embark on is not some pseudo-state of mind. One where you're having to trick yourself into believing that you're happy all the time. Rather, this is a calling toward the highest and best use of your life. A life marked by surrender and submission to the God who created you, while putting your full trust in how He says to live it out rightly.

All of this is summed up in the biblical expression of "obedience". Whoever or whatever you obey becomes your god and determines the fate of your future. (We are all submitting to some sort of code for life, whether we realize it or not.)

Pursuing genuine joy, purpose and meaning flows from doing what Jesus did and what He told us to do. He designed us to experience our greatest level of fulfillment and well being when we follow His lead. This could not be simpler in concept. Admittedly though, understanding this is the easy part of the equation. It's the "living it out" part that trips us up. Oh, if we could only see that the reward makes the effort seem so trivial by comparison! How different would our lives be?

Grounding this even more into reality, Jesus does not promise a joy that is devoid of trials. What He does offer however, is a joy that is activated in even the worst of trials. The Apostle Peter explains:

> **This brings you great joy, although you may have to suffer for a short time in various trials.**
>
> **Such trials show the proven character of your faith... and will bring praise and glory and honor when Jesus Christ is revealed.**
>
> **You have not seen Him, but you love Him. You do not see Him now but you believe in Him, and so you rejoice with an indescribable and glorious joy .**
>
> **1 Peter 1:6-8 NET**

Peter is telling us that a Christ-centered joy becomes a powerful tool, even in the midst of life's toughest battles. However, we're not talking about a spiteful or vengeful type of joy—that would not be joy at all. Rather this is the proof of your life as authentically being lived out. One in which our joy is not rooted in this world, therefore nothing and no one in this world can steal it from us.

So what happens if and when you get knocked off this path towards the joy that Christ provides? Perhaps this is you right now? King David shows us the heart and resolve needed behind your next steps:

> Restore to me the joy **of your salvation, and make me willing to obey you.**
> **Psalm 51:12 NLT**

Yes. Joy can be restored! Especially in a season of recovery, we see that surrender to God's will is the impetus for joy being restored back into your life. Pick yourself up. Dust yourself off. Keep moving forward.

Do you struggle with your desire to obey God? That's alright, you're in good company. Even David—who was accredited as being one after God's own heart—had to pray that God would "make me willing to obey you."

David, in another psalm (or song) of his, reveals yet another connection between joy and obeying God:

> **You will show me the path of life;** In Your presence is fullness of joy; **At Your right hand are pleasures forevermore.**
> **Psalms 16:11 NKJV**

Herein lies the unobstructed path to enter ultimate pleasure: Christ's way is the only way to experience a full and joyous life. At best, this world can only offer temporary versions and at worst harmful counterfeits. True and real and lasting joy can only be found in Christ.

We want to challenge you with your next steps: Make up your mind to be open-hearted to the path that lies ahead of you.

Get ready to be amazed at the transformation you'll experience inside your own soul as we move through the themes of *seeking, surrender, serving* and *sharing.*

If you are willing to put these teachings into action, you will develop the skill of accessing ***JOY ON COMMAND***.

1.0 | JOY IN SEEKING

JOY IN SEEKING GOD

So will My word be which goes out of My mouth; It will not return to Me empty, without accomplishing what I desire, and without succeeding in the purpose for which I sent it.

For you will go out with joy and be led in peace...

Isaiah 55:11-12 NASB

1.1 | COME AND SEE

"Come and see," He (Jesus) said. It was about four o'clock in the afternoon when they went with Him to the place where He was staying, and they remained with Him the rest of the day.
John 1:39 NLT

Jesus invites us. *All* of us.

We are given an open invitation to embark on a life-long journey of placing our trust in Him. God is so incredibly patient with each of us. More than we may realize. How so? Because even before the commitment to the actual journey, Jesus challenges us to simply take a small step with Him. We are lovingly dared to check it out first.

The narrative in John 1 shows us how easily accessible Christ can be. His first soon-to-be disciples, Andrew and Peter, are the ones mentioned above in this exchange. Saying in effect, "Let's hang out!" Jesus invites them to where He was staying. Then they spend the rest of the day enjoying each other's company. Could you imagine what it would be like getting this kind of face time with Jesus?

Maybe you've not yet come to realize how approachable God makes Himself. Listen to the first words mentioned in the Bible, that come out of Jesus' mouth to those who are curious about Him:

Jesus looked around and saw them following.

> **"What do you want?" He asked them. They replied, "Rabbi" (which means "Teacher"), "where are you staying?"**
>
> **"Come and see," He said.**
> **John 1:38-39 NLT**

Remarkable! The first thing God offers to those who are genuinely curious about Him is the question:

"What do YOU want from Me?"

He doesn't start out with a monologue to impress you. (And He, of course, doesn't need to.) Rather, He hits right to the heart of the human need to be heard and understood.

Have you ever truly asked yourself this question? What do you (or would you) want out of an authentic relationship with the God of this universe? What would be a meaningful enough exchange with the one who came to die for your sins? The mind boggles at the very idea of such a question!

Another quick note from Peter and Andrew was their apparent willingness to learn. They honored Christ as a teacher and humbled themselves to show their own ability to be taught. Some refer to this as their *teachability* or their *coach-ability*.

How coachable are you? Would you give God a legitimate chance to show you who He really is?

Once one says *yes* to Jesus' invitation to come and see, it's often difficult for them to keep this encounter to themselves. Look at what happens next with Peter and Andrew's friend Philip and later still, their friend Nathanael:

> **Philip found Nathanael and told him, "We have found the one Moses wrote about in the Law, and about whom the prophets also wrote—Jesus of**

Nazareth, the son of Joseph."

"Nazareth! Can anything good come from there?" Nathanael asked. "Come and see," said Philip.

John 1:45-46 NIV

Have you ever had an extraordinary dish at a restaurant and couldn't help but post a picture of it on social media to let the world see? Or perhaps a movie, youtube video or tv show that you just had to recommend to a friend? We do this in hopes that they'll be as interested as we were, so that we can talk about it together.

This is exactly what we see happening through Philip's conversation with Nathanael. He's so drawn in by his interaction with Jesus that he couldn't help but bring his friend into the same experience. That's a good friend.

How many times have you attempted to convince your family or friends of something you've encountered that was really outstanding? Did they doubt you when you tried to explain it to them? This phenomena is nothing new. This is part of the human condition. A way that we tend to guard ourselves from being let down or disappointed.

Jesus knows all this and yet, still offers great patience in our reluctance. You can read the rest of the above exchange (see John 1:45-51), but suffice it to say that Jesus doesn't miss a beat with Nathaniel and even gives him a little more proof to help ease his doubts.

He has a way of meeting people—like you and I—right where we are. Conversely, we also have to be willing to give Him a hearing and this is where the psalmist can help us:

Taste and see that the LORD is good; blessed is the

one who takes refuge in Him.
Psalm 34:8 NIV

In many ice cream shops today, they offer a sample spoon. They do this so that you're not committed to the whole scoop before you know what it tastes like. In a very similar fashion, God offers us the same sample of Himself. Being that as it may, let's not let this illustration diminish the importance of this decision to "come and see" Jesus.

Whatever or whoever you take refuge in is, in fact, your God. Who or what you ultimately place your faith in, will ultimately determine your destiny.

Take Jesus up on His offer to come and see how He can change your life, your eternity, your world view and your overall well being.

△△△

1. My TAKE AWAY from this chapter is...

2. This chapter makes me GRATEFUL because...

3. I will TAKE ACTION for this by...

1.2 | RECEIVE GOD LIKE A CHILD

Let the children come to me. Don't stop them! For the Kingdom of God belongs to those who are like these children.

I tell you the truth, anyone who doesn't receive the Kingdom of God like a child **will never enter it.**

Luke 18:16-17 NLT

Being one of the most precious scenes in Christ's ministry, we enter a crowd of families and their children. Jesus' patience and kindness are on full display as He interacts with them all. In the preceding verse (v. 15), we are also clued in that it was actually the parents who were bringing their children to be blessed by Jesus. Fantastic parenting!

The greatest thing a mother or father could ever do for their child is to introduce them to Jesus!

As the scene progresses, we next see an exchange that we would do well to take a moment and think through its implications: Jesus' disciples are seen disparaging these parent's efforts by reasoning that Jesus is too important a public figure to be busied by children. Before we get upset with them, is it not true that we do the same sort of thing?

Have you ever felt like you were bothering God?

Perhaps you have been hesitant because a particular prayer need seemed too small to bring to God or too big to entrust to Him? Or maybe, just maybe, it is we who simply don't want to bother with the exercise of coming to our Heavenly Father as a child. The tragedy of this is that we truly end up missing out. Why?

Because God wants to "wow" His children!

Of course, we are not being called by Christ to be immature (see 1 Corinthians 13:11) in our faith journey. That is called being child*ish*. Big difference from child*like*.

There is an altogether playful and beautiful sense of humility in a child's eyes, mind and heart. We are to rescue this sense of childlike wonderment as we consider the expansive power and extensive love of the Father.

> **So anyone who becomes** as humble as this little child is the greatest **in the Kingdom of Heaven.**
> **Matthew 18:4 NLT**

Children (up to a certain age) are the ideal combination of total trust, utter humility, and animated anticipation. Everything a young child encounters is a new and stimulating learning experience, thus making them all the more impressionable at younger ages. How receptive are you to the will, the teachings, and the promises of God?

Have you lost your childlike edge in your openness with Christ?

As we grow older, both skepticism and even cynicism become all too easy a temptation. When left unchecked, it can be allowed to grow within us like a cancer. To be fair, this is because we've all experienced let downs in life, and even betrayals. In fact, disappointments like these are one of the chief reasons that we often lose our childlike faith. We're told (or we tell ourselves) to "grow up."

Maturity has its proper place, but like the parents that were seeking Jesus to bless their children, we also should seek out trustworthy peers and mentors that will continue to stir up our sense of awe and wonder towards God.

Paul gives a glowing endorsement regarding Timothy while also depicting the value of this childlike faith:

But you know of his proven character, that he served with me in the furtherance of the gospel like a child serving **his father.**
Philippians 2:22 NASB

Consider these concepts mentioned above by Paul: "proven character" and "loyal service." These being the result of a childlike trust and receptivity to moving the gospel forward.

If not careful, we are in danger of picking up some bad habits along the way that could interrupt, disrupt and even corrupt how we look at God.

When we lose sense of His greatness, we run to other things for a "fix." Temporary solutions that ultimately leave us even more empty and dissatisfied. Then (if left unchecked) comes the inevitable spiral down to an unforgiving and tragic rock-bottom.

However, with power in His wings to rescue, the Holy Spirit provides the revelation and encouragement to start fresh again. Being made "brand new" trades upon the currency of redemption, that yields new hopes and strengthened resolve.

The question then is, "How can we stay wonderfully aware and receptive to God and all He has for us?" Peter speaks to this very matter when he says:

Therefore, rid yourselves of all malice, all deceit, hypocrisy, envy, and all slander.

Like newborn infants, desire the pure **milk of the**

word, so that by it you may grow up into your salvation, if you have tasted that the Lord is good.
1 Peter 2:1-3 CSB

There you have it. If we continually allow God the chance to wow us, He consistently will. If we pursue the purity of the Holy Spirit and the undiluted essence of the gospel, our lives will be filled with awestruck wonder. As Peter says, we must work to rid ourselves of the contrivances that would otherwise hinder a deeper, more fulfilling relationship with God.

Newborns are insatiably hungry and in need of constant care and attention. So also should our desires be towards our Heavenly Father. Don't think you're bothering Him.

God is deeply compassionate about reaching out to those who willingly receive Him like a child.

△△△

1. My TAKE AWAY from this chapter is…

2. This chapter makes me GRATEFUL because…

3. I will TAKE ACTION for this by…

1.3 | SEEK GOD'S KINGDOM FIRST

But seek first the kingdom of God and His righteousness, and all these things shall be added to you.
Matthew 6:33 NKJV

What are you pursuing most in life?

Have you ever intentionally taken the time needed to pause and meditate on this? Jesus prescribes this preeminent formula, that when lived out, allows for all the other things in our lives to fall into their proper place. He issues this command in the troubled space of our worries and anxieties (which we'll touch on in future sessions.)

Referred to as an "if/then" promise, we learn that if we seek His Kingdom, His will, His Word—in essence, if we seek Him—then all the other needs in our lives would be fulfilled. They would be "added" to us. God loves to add and to multiply to those who seek Him first.

We can see the proposition of this promise laid out many centuries earlier when God spoke to a young King Solomon. God gave Solomon an opportunity to ask whatever he wanted from The Lord. Solomon requested godly wisdom to govern in a way that would honor the God of Israel, as well as his own father's legacy. The Lord honored this desire and told Solomon that because he didn't make a selfish request (riches, fame, etc), that He'd go ahead and throw in all the other perks. So much so that it is said there was no richer or wiser king in all the history of

Israel as was King Solomon. (See 1 Kings 3.)

For some peculiar reason, it is difficult for some Christians to believe that God wants the very best for you. He wants more for your life, not less. He has bigger dreams for you. Oftentimes it is the temptation of things owning us, rather than us owning things, that trips us up along the way. This is precisely what takes us out of alignment with God's will.

One way Jesus exposes our true motives is to look no further than our own finances:

> **Fear not, little flock, for** it is your Father's good pleasure to give you the Kingdom...
>
> **For where your treasure is, there will your heart be also.**
> **Luke 12:32,34 ESV**

You can tell what you care about most by simply taking an honest inventory of where you invest your time, talent and treasure.

God doesn't want to withhold His Kingdom and His blessing from His kids. In fact, God thoroughly enjoys pouring out benefit upon His followers. The caveat is that many times He will, in fact, withhold from us when He sees that the blessing was all we were really after in the end. Blessing, when not properly stewarded, can quickly become a curse. It is a tempting snare to build up our own kingdom at the expense of His.

It is said that, "Absolute power corrupts absolutely."

Paul warns the church at Galatia of the results of not seeking God's Kingdom above their own desires:

> **When you follow the desires of your sinful nature, the results are very clear...**

Let me tell you again, as I have before, that anyone living that sort of life will not inherit the Kingdom of God.

Galatians 5:19, 21 NLT

Our sinful, fallen, human nature is our biggest enemy.

When we put ourselves first, the disastrous results are as predictable as they are inescapable. Without even realizing it, we make ourselves our own god when we do such things. This is why it is imperative that we learn the discipline of looking through the lens of eternity when making directional changes in our lives. We should ask ourselves:

"How will this glorify God?" And...

"Is what I'm about to do going to prioritize God's Kingdom or my own?"

To add balance, understand that healthy growth in the ranks of an entrepreneurial endeavor or a promotion at the job can be a good thing when used for God's glory. It is incredible when we see God's Kingdom flourishing on earth, because those who are willing participants flourish as well. Ironically enough, history bears witness time and time again that this can happen even in the midst of the worst kinds of trials:

Dear brothers and sisters, we can't help but thank God for you, because your faith is flourishing and your love for one another is growing...

And God will use this persecution to show His justice and to make you worthy of His Kingdom, for which you are suffering.

2 Thessalonians 1:3, 5 NLT

When seeking God's Kingdom first, it's been said that, "the set back is actually the set up" for something even greater.

This was Paul's encouragement to the Thessalonian church. Trial by fire has a way of burning out the impurities while making us a more refined, purer vessel that can then receive the best from God. We become more humble, more wise, more focused and more thankful.

As we begin to prioritize God's Kingdom, He begins to change the very nature of our desires. We slowly stop craving the fame, fortune and power of this life and trade those things for the treasures that look far beyond this life. Leveraging the temporal resources we've been given, we begin to pursue things that satisfy an eternal effect and reward.

Whatever may be your current state and status in life, seek first God's Kingdom. Practice towards a personal worthiness of His eternal Kingdom. Then watch things also begin to change in the here and now.

ΔΔΔ

1. My TAKE AWAY from this chapter is...

2. This chapter makes me GRATEFUL because...

3. I will TAKE ACTION for this by...

1.4 | ENTER THROUGH THE NARROW DOOR

Enter by the narrow gate (door). **For the gate is wide and the way is easy that leads to destruction, and those who enter by it are many.**

For the gate is narrow **and the way is hard that leads to life, and those who find it are few.**
Matthew 7:13-14 ESV

Many of us have survived the embarrassing confusion of entering an unfamiliar building with a maze of long hallways jutting out in multiple directions. Each one of these with way too many possible doors leading into way too many rooms. Most of them carrying similar markings (and some times, none at all) leaving one stumped as to which door is the correct door.

Similarly, this type of scenario plays out on a far grander scale in the spiritual realm. Picking among the vast array of world-views and belief systems available could quickly become overwhelming. When chosen irresponsibly, they could even lead to rationalizing corrupt and often misguided moral decisions.

Then enters Jesus, with His unmistakable claim at deity in the passage above. He has no problem saying, "I'm different from all the other doors. Don't go the other ways that are false and lead to destruction. I'm the door you're looking for."

The Apostle John records a similar occasion for this claim and peppers in a few other ingredients:

> I am the Door; **anyone who** enters through Me **will be saved (and will live forever), and will go in and out (freely), and find pasture (spiritual security).**
>
> John 10:9 AMP

We learn here that it is through Christ alone that salvation, freedom and security all intersect at one commonplace. Saying "yes" to Him opens the eternal door that stands above the worldly capacities for corrosion and corruption.

With Christ, we experience a call towards free, exhilarating exploration. At the same time, we enjoy the peaceful rest of finally getting to settle somewhere securely without fear of the enemy.

Have you ever noticed the unspoken rules for entering doors that lead into different social constructs? If it's a fun party, you put on your biggest smile and your best sing-song voice as you greet everyone. Conversely, if it's a funeral, you approach with a respectful reverence. Still yet, if it's an important business meeting, you enter the door with your most convincing "game face."

With that in mind, listen to how the psalmist encourages us to enter through this door:

> Enter into His gates with thanksgiving,**And** into His courts with praise. **Be thankful to Him, and bless His name.**
>
> **For the Lord is good; His mercy is everlasting, And His truth endures to all generations.**
>
> Psalm 100:4-5 NKJV

When you give your thoughts over to all that God has done for you, how could this not be your response?

And while many believe this should be our hearts as we enter into our church buildings, this passage also represents the exceedingly joyous occasion that it is to enter His Presence. Posture yourself with thankfulness, praise and blessing to God because of the everlasting and enduring nature of His goodness, mercy and truth!

Permission to enter through the singular door that Jesus provides should certainly elicit eager anticipation. As benefactors, we are granted access to all that God has for us:

> **Blessed are those who wash their robes. They will be permitted to enter through the gates of the city and eat the fruit from the tree of life.**
> **Revelation 22:14 NLT**

Once and for all, we are washed through the precious, innocent blood of Jesus. Through Him we've exchanged our "filthy rags" for His righteousness (see Isaiah 64:6).

This *salvation* operates in three phases:

First, *justification* speaks to the initial forgiveness of our sins by Jesus, found in our repentance to Him.

Second, *sanctification* speaks to the purifying and refining work of the Holy Spirit throughout the life of the believer.

Third, there is the *glorification* that we are all awaiting to experience when we are changed in the "blink of an eye." Where we'll also enjoy our eternally upgraded bodies, as well as the unimpeded view of Heaven and our Savior. (See 1 Corinthians 15:51-53.)

The restorative power of entering through the narrow door

also indicates our regaining access to the "Tree of Life." Many believe this is literally referring to the tree tragically lost in Eden millennia ago, while others believe this is metaphorically pointing towards the full enjoyment of the Presence of God. Whatever the matter, I think of a line from the old hymn, "Won't it be wonderful there!"

As you consider entering through the narrow door, what should be taken into account is that Jesus is big enough for the whole world to walk through and into Heaven. The door is "narrow" because it represents a clear, unambiguous choice. One that we must all make.

In our hearts, whoever we determine Jesus to be makes an eternity of difference.

ΔΔΔ

1. My TAKE AWAY from this chapter is...

2. This chapter makes me GRATEFUL because...

3. I will TAKE ACTION for this by...

1.5 | REPENT

"The time promised by God has come at last!" He announced. "The Kingdom of God is near!

Repent of your sins and believe the Good News!"
Mark 1:15 NLT

This bold declaration comes right after the disturbing announcement that John-the-Baptist had just been thrown in jail. John had also been directing all his former disciples to now begin following Jesus. He knew he had faithfully completed his task as Messiah's herald and that his time was short.

Jesus then enters Mark's gospel account essentially declaring, "I'm here! I've made myself close and accessible to humankind. Turn away from that which caused you to turn away from God."

This was no small statement that Jesus was making. In effect, He was announcing the fulfillment of centuries of prophecy. The good news was that God was now again making Himself tangible and approachable to all. Ever since the sin of Adam and Eve in the garden, this had not been previously possible. He was now urging them that they had what they needed—in Him—to turn away from lifestyles that were in opposition to God.

The connection of repentance to the news that, "God's Kingdom is near," is unmistakable and clear. Without repentance, we cannot and will not enjoy the benefits of God's Presence.

The Apostle Paul explains the bridge that repentance builds between us and God:

> **For** godly grief produces a repentance **that leads to salvation without regret, whereas worldly grief produces death.**
>
> **For see what earnestness this godly grief has produced in you, but also what eagerness to clear yourselves.**
>
> 2 Corinthians 7:10-11 ESV

There is a fundamental distinction made between *conviction* and *condemnation.*

Understanding that we grieve the Holy Spirit when we sin is meant to lead us to back to Him through the contrition of repentance. This act of humility before God, as we ask for forgiveness and plot out a new course, produces new life in us. Whereas *worldly* grief is hopeless, a genuine *godly* grief is in stead hope-filled.

The reason this is true is because it causes in us the desire, effect and result of wanting to clear this guilt. In addition, we gain appreciation that this is even possible in the first place.

Have you ever just wanted to feel completely clean and cleared of guilt, sin and shame?

Of course, we understand we cannot do this through any practice of self-righteousness, but only through the righteousness of God revealed in the death, burial and resurrection of Jesus Christ. We will learn in other chapters that Christ's clothing us in His righteousness—through repentance—is simultaneously the means by which we clear any sin in our ledger.

Peter takes this even further:

> Repent **therefore and be converted, that your sins**

may be blotted out, so that times of refreshing
may come from the Presence of the Lord,
Acts 3:19 NKJV

So we see there is a conversion that takes place at the altar of repentance. We certainly understand this to be true initially when a sinner first gives his or her life to God for salvation.

Consider this however: repentance is a lifestyle more so than a single act. Explained in pastor-speak: "Living your life at the altar, alters you." Repentance changes you in the most fundamental of ways, while also posturing your heart toward a state of constant humility before God.

There is a refreshment that is to be experienced from having your name and your sin cleared before God. Humility in His Presence gives way to boldness in your worship and prayer before Him. God does not want you living with a spirit of heaviness because of the weight of sin. He wants to refresh you to your core and point you in the direction of His will.

Jesus also imbues you, through the power of the Holy Spirit, so that you can be a living witness of His grace and mercy. God wants people to see Him through you. Luke records this matter-of-factly:

Prove by the way you live that you have repented of
your sins and turned to God...
Luke 3:8 NLT

Our repentance should be verifiable, provable and tangible to ourselves and to others.

Have you ever witnessed the radical change in someone's life that proved that they had indeed turned from the old lies of their old lives? The most beautiful way that a person can testify to the reality of God is through the realness of their repentance.

If you are wanting to experience complete joy in your life, repentance is one of the most important keys you can use to access the fulfillment that frees your mind, heart and spirit. As the song says, "In His Presence, is fullness of joy."

△△△

1. My TAKE AWAY from this chapter is...

2. This chapter makes me GRATEFUL because...

3. I will TAKE ACTION for this by...

1.6 | RECEIVE THE HOLY SPIRIT

So Jesus said to them again, "Peace to you! As the Father has sent Me, I also send you."

And when He had said this, He breathed on them, and said to them "Receive the Holy Spirit."
John 20:21-22 NKJV

Can you imagine the headspace that Jesus' disciples must have been in at this very moment?

They're all still reeling after the brutal execution of their Teacher. Then, they had just discovered the earth-shattering truth that no one knows where their Rabbi's body has gone. If all that wasn't enough, one of the women followers was seemingly hysterical, trying to convince them that she just saw their friend Jesus...alive! All the scrambling and the confusion must have been overwhelming!

Finally, they all arrive together in a single room to try to catch their breath (which was also locked because they were all still frightened out of their minds) while trying to make heads or tails out of this information overload.

Suddenly, out of nowhere, Jesus appears! And every anxious feeling they had up to that moment began to slowly melt away.

Isn't that just like Jesus? Our world could be totally off-kilter, not knowing which way is up or down, mass confusion and hysteria in expectation of the worse possible case scenario. And then, Jesus appears. His Presence brings His peace, the type of peace that passes all understanding.

Next, Jesus wastes no time in bringing clarity to His disciples (soon to be upgraded to "Apostles") that the mission of His death, burial and resurrection was finished. He was now calling on them to carry this gospel forward as their life's mission. True and total forgiveness of humanity's sins was now possible because of the completed work of Jesus Christ.

Even more curious, Jesus breathes on His disciples, pointing them back full-circle to prophecy. This was the same initial breath of the Holy Spirit that went into Adam and Eve at the dawn of humanity. He goes on to explain a little later:

> **But you will** receive power when the Holy Spirit comes upon you. **And you will be My witnesses, telling people about Me everywhere.**
>
> **Acts 1:8 NLT**

God empowers us with such a precious promise for a very clear purpose: Not for our own fame, fortune or vainglory but rather, to be His witnesses. Yes, it's that simple. We who have received the Spirit of God have work to do. Consecrating everything to God, from the everyday mundane tasks, as well as the happiest and saddest moments of our lives. This is precisely how we bring glory to God.

How often are you pointing those in your circle to the love and life you've found in Christ? Are you aware and do you know how to activate the empowerment of the Holy Spirit in your witness? The Apostle Peter presents the best teaching on the starting point, in addition to the lifestyle of the spiritually empowered believer:

> **Peter said to them, "Repent, and each of you be baptized in the name of Jesus Christ for the forgiveness of your sins; and you will** receive the

gift of the Holy Spirit.

For the promise is for you and your children and for all who are far away, as many as the Lord our God will call to Himself."

Acts 2:38-39 NASB

Peter's sermon above reveals a most fundamental key with which we gain access to the Holy Spirit. We learned the power of this in our previous session. Repentance is the prerequisite to a true capacity to receive the Holy Spirit. There must be the deepest and genuine heart's desire to turn away from sin and turn to God before we are able to receive what He has for us.

The role of water baptism is also helpful in context. For our purposes today, we understand that baptism is the way we "outwardly declare what we've inwardly confessed." Our faith is meant to be expressed publicly. When we are water baptized, we are symbolically identifying with the death, burial and resurrection of Jesus.

Let's also carefully note that the promise of the Holy Spirit is a "gift" and "promise" that is perpetual in nature. It is something you "get to have" rather than "have to get." Additionally, it was not only meant for those alive at the time of the disciples. One simply needs to read verse 39 to see this was meant for all people at all times until the return of our Lord.

There is something special that takes place in our souls when we are open to receiving the Holy Spirit. Paul speaks to this when he says:

When you believed, you were marked in Him with a seal, the promised Holy Spirit, who is a deposit guaranteeing our inheritance until the redemption of those who are God's possession...

24

Just like a king would seal a letter with his signet as a display of the authority to the words written within, Jesus placed his seal on us. The authority of The Word has marked us safe in a way that the enemy has no lien on our souls. The Holy Spirit both heightens our awareness of the schemes of the enemy as well as empowers us to overcome his devices of deceit and despondency.

What is most elegant about the passage above is when one realizes that this gift is only a "deposit of the good things to come!" Said another way, this gift is only the beginning for all that God has in store for those who receive His Holy Spirit.

△△△

1. My TAKE AWAY from this chapter is...

2. This chapter makes me GRATEFUL because...

3. I will TAKE ACTION for this by...

1.7 | PRAY THIS WAY

...your Father knows what you need before you ask Him.

So pray this way:
Matthew 6:8-9 NET

On the heels of Jesus mentoring His disciples against being hypocritical or giving "vain repetition" to their prayers (Matthew 6:5-7), we are given a gem of a teaching session on what the model of God-honoring prayer looks like. Luke also adds a layer to this setting by revealing that one of Jesus' disciples had the good sense to ask, "Lord, teach us to pray..." (See Luke 11:1.)

Reminding them all first of the love and care of their Heavenly Father, Jesus proceeds to lay out an exquisitely simple prayer guide for them. Again, it is to be understood that this is not meant to be mindlessly repeated, but rather to be a thought-provoking journey of prayerful meditation.

Jesus begins with teaching pure worship:

Our Father in Heaven, Hallowed be Your Name.
Matthew 6:9 NKJV

Have you ever taken a moment to just bask in the holiness of God? Have you ever tried to visualize your Heavenly Father shining His light of love and acknowledgment on you from Heaven? One should feel so honored to be allowed proximity and access to His Presence and authority!

To be "hallowed" is to "set something apart as special, without parallel or equal." Does the Name of Jesus hold this level of sincere reverence in your heart and life?

The next line further expands on this idea and connects it to God as The Supreme Authority over Heaven and Earth:

Your Kingdom come. Your will be done on earth as it is in Heaven.
Matthew 6:10 NKJV

Covering all of heaven and earth, this line of the prayer is exponentially eternal and infinitely expansive in its scope. It's also very personal. Consider for a moment God's will in your own life. It's easy to pray His will over everything else, but ask yourself if you are truly willing to surrender your own will first?

Praying this encourages us that there will be a "new Heaven and a new Earth." At the same time, our attention is also being centered towards our current journey through this broken creation. We believe Him when He says, "I will make all things new!"

Give us this day our daily bread.
Matthew 6:11 NKJV

Many commentators have noted that this "daily bread" speaks to more than just physical food. We are to daily request and express gratitude for spiritual, relational, financial and emotional sustenance. We trust God for our daily supply.

And forgive us our debts, As we forgive our debtors.
Matthew 6:12 NKJV

Being a prayer that spans across many layers of the human experience, this one is the most bittersweet. Who doesn't love being forgiven of falling short, missing the target or crossing a line we shouldn't have? That's the sweet part. There is nothing like feeling forgiven!

Conversely, we learn with this prayer that the measure of our receiving forgiveness is dependent on how authentically we've forgiven others. That's a tough pill to swallow!

Have you ever paused at this point in The Lord's Prayer to consider those whom you need to forgive? Be encouraged by knowing that truly forgiving others brings with it a joyous release, many times over the feeling of being forgiven yourself.

And do not lead us into temptation, But deliver us from the evil one.
Matthew 6:13 NKJV

Wisely moving from the power of forgiveness, we now see Jesus guiding us into guarding our heart, mind, body and spirit from further damage. We know that God would never tempt us Himself, but rather, it is our own evil tendencies and desires that seek to separate us from God's path. (See James 1:13-15).

So first comes the prayer to resist the sin nature in ourselves. Then comes the resistance to the enticements and deceit of the enemy of our souls. We've been given authority over the power of the enemy. Through prayers like this, we posture and position our awareness to be on watch.

For Yours is the Kingdom and the power and the glory forever. Amen.
Matthew 6:13 NKJV

Concluding this prayer guide full circle, we arrive where we began. We lavish worship on our great God! We learn the power of sandwiching our needs in between our praise. Not because God can be flattered, but because it keeps our flesh in a place of surrender to His will and authority. We were created with an innate desire to rejoice over our Savior in His Presence.

This type of prayer is how we command joy in our lives!

△△△

1. My TAKE AWAY from this chapter is...

2. This chapter makes me GRATEFUL because...

3. I will TAKE ACTION for this by...

1.8 | GIVE GOD WHAT BELONGS TO HIM

"Well, then," Jesus said, "give to Caesar what belongs to Caesar, and give to God what belongs to God." **His reply completely amazed them.**
Mark 12:17 NLT

Ever been in a conversation where the other person asked a spiteful and deceitful question? One that was meant to put you in a sticky, no-win situation?

This was one of those moments for Jesus. (See verses 13-15.) The religious leaders of His day were looking for any legal charges they could bring against Him. Their only problem was that everyone was amazed at this man and held Him in high regard as a true prophet sent from God. This passage, containing the command to "Give God what belongs to God," holds within it, one of the best one-liners by Jesus to His nay-sayers. One which also continues to hold all of us in perpetual wonderment of Jesus' wisdom and wit.

Here, Jesus models a powerful method for cutting through the schemes of the wicked and those not genuine in their curiosity of Him. Rather than allowing Himself to be painted into a corner by these Pharisees, He responds back with an equally provocative counter-challenge:

"Shew me a penny. Whose image and superscription hath it?" They answered and said,

"Caesar's."

And He said unto them, "Render therefore unto Caesar the things which be Caesar's, and unto God the things which be God's."
Luke 20:24-25 KJV

There are a few things to note from the above exchange. Jesus' cleverness exposed what we call a "categorical fallacy" on the part of the religious leaders. Uncovering this error was simply meant to demonstrate that what belongs to Caesar—the taxes and the money with which to pay them—did belong, in fact, to Caesar. The issue of whether or not the Jews should be exempt from taxes was irrelevant as well as starting a disingenuous debate altogether.

Even more disappointing, these Pharisees missed the greatest possible opportunity for a follow up question. They could (and should) have asked, "Well then, what belongs to God?" Of which I am certain Jesus would have replied, "Good question. Whose image and superscription is upon you?"

We know from the very beginning of the Bible, that we were created in "Imago Dei." That is, in the Image of Almighty God. Astonishingly, we also learn that we bear the "superscription" or the epigraph of the Lord's written Word on our hearts. (See Romans 2:15-16.) This is why we are to love God with all that we are (which our next chapter will explore), because we are made to be mini-reflections of His glory. His undeniable imprint is upon us all.

So, because we owe all that we are to Him, we belong to Him.

Still, there are those that deny this. Accordingly, these are the same that also refuse to give God the honor and glory which belongs to Him. They do this to their own self-harm:

> **...since the creation of the world... His eternal power and divine nature, have been clearly perceived, being understood by what has been made...**
>
> **For even though they knew God,** they did not honor Him as God or give thanks, **but they became futile in their reasonings, and their senseless hearts were darkened.**
> Romans 1:20-21 NASB

There is a deep darkness that encompasses those who are "willingly ignorant" to the natural law that undeniably points to a Creator and Designer.

As the passage explains, once one denies these fundamental truths, their reasoning further unravels into unlivable futility. Inside a rebellious heart, one can simply read the rest of this chapter in Romans to see the line of despair that leads inevitably to destruction.

Though this may be the path for the rest of the world that is in opposition to Christ, it is not the path for those who are on the quest to experience a fullness of joy. In this journey, we are already witnessing the differences in our hearts, minds, relationships and otherwise with every new "yes" we say to Christ's teachings.

This endeavor also points us to the evidence that our bodies are to become the fulfillment of the Old Testament temple, destined to house the Holy Spirit:

> **Now,** give your heart and your soul to seek Jehovah your God... **rise and build... bring in the ark of the covenant... and the holy vessels of God, to the house that is built to the name of Jehovah.**
> 1 Chronicles 22:19 YLT

With this passage in mind, the Apostle Peter connects the dots to further reveal that we, "like living stones are being built up as a spiritual house, to be a holy priesthood, to offer spiritual sacrifices acceptable to God through Jesus Christ." (See 1 Peter 2:5.)

You are a part of this *house*. His Church.

So we understand that as we develop the discipline to rise and build and bring our lives before God, that we are indeed "giving God what belongs to Him."

△△△

1. My TAKE AWAY from this chapter is...

2. This chapter makes me GRATEFUL because...

3. I will TAKE ACTION for this by...

1.9 | LOVE GOD WITH ALL YOUR BEING

"Teacher, which commandment in the law is the greatest?"

Jesus said to him, "Love the Lord your God with all your heart, with all your soul, and with all your mind.'

This is the first and greatest commandment."
Matthew 22:36-38 NET

Jesus teaches that you can sum up all the other commands through the lens of this one. Said another way, when we get this right, the others will naturally (or maybe *supernaturally)* fall in line.

Again, as mentioned in previous chapters, this teaching comes as Christ's response to a gambit of questions from religious leaders meaning to trap Him. Ironically, we have His opposers to thank for helping us mine some of the most valuable lessons that Jesus ever gives.

Being even more fascinating, understand that every Jew of Jesus' day was already aware of this command as it was the same given Israel centuries prior, when Moses was leading them. Christ was simply reaffirming the singular command that should have already been central to their culture.

We remember this same instruction originally being spoken

through Moses to Israel as they are preparing to enter the promised land:

> **And you must** love the LORD your God with all your heart, all your soul, and all your strength.
>
> **And you must commit yourselves** wholeheartedly **to these commands that I am giving you today.**
> **Deuteronomy 6:5-6 NLT**

Previously we've learned that because we humans bear the image of Almighty God, we are indebted to give back to God what belongs to Him. And what belongs to God is the totality of our love and commitment.

Does your love for God flow from the very core of who you are? Would you say that you are committed wholeheartedly to what God commands us as disciples? One's level of love and commitment are quite often in direct correlation to the level of trust placed in its object. Do you trust that His commands were meant to bring you true joy rather than just a sorrowful burden?

We see that to "love God with all your being" was designed to fully engage the spirit, soul and body. Doing this not just when convenient, but even to the extent of our daily practice.

Listen to how we are to constantly practice these life-giving commands, so that we do not slip or falter:

> Repeat them again and again **to your children.** Talk about them **when you are at home and when you are on the road, when you are going to bed and when you are getting up.**
>
> Tie them **to your hands and** wear them **on your forehead as reminders.**

Write them on the doorposts of your house and on your gates.
Deuteronomy 6:7-9 NLT

It's been said that "love is a verb."

This is certainly the case as stated above. Making the decision to be a follower of Christ was meant to be expressed as a lifestyle of committed devotion. A devotion that should permeate every area of our lives. This is not something that can be compartmentalized for an hour on Sundays.

Half-hearted devotion is not the way genuine love works.

When love is wholehearted, there's no need for a reminder to talk about it, think about it, write about it, repeat it and so on. It becomes something you enjoy and anticipate practicing mini-expressions of throughout your day.

Loving Christ with all that you are carries with it its own reward. God is the epitome of love itself (1 John 14:6) and therefore responds to love.

Listen to this if/then promise spoken from God, again through Moses:

So if you faithfully obey the commands I am giving you today—to love the Lord your God and to serve Him with all your heart and with all your soul—

then I will send... so that you may gather in...

I will provide... and you will eat and be satisfied.
Deuteronomy 11:13-15 NIV

While there are no conditions to God's love, there are however conditions upon whom His favor and blessing rests. It is always beautiful to see how God miraculously sends His blessing and provision—even in the darkest of hours—to those who love Him completely and who obey Him fully.

Our Savior is the only one who can ultimately and totally satisfy the needs of the spirit, soul, mind, heart and body. This is why we must devote to Him all of these components that make up the entirety our being.

$$\triangle\triangle\triangle$$

1. My TAKE AWAY from this chapter is...

2. This chapter makes me GRATEFUL because...

3. I will TAKE ACTION for this by...

1.10 | WORSHIP IN SPIRIT AND TRUTH

The time is coming—indeed it's here now—when true worshipers will worship the Father in spirit and in truth. **The Father is looking for those who will** worship Him that way.

John 4:23 NLT

We enter into this narrative at its very crescendo in the verse above. Jesus is revealing, to this Samaritan "woman at the well," that He is the long-awaited and promised Messiah.

While we may have the power of hindsight, can you imagine how provocative a statement this was to be making? In context, Jesus was answering this woman's questions as to who had the rightful access to the God of Israel and by which means to accurately worship Him.

Additionally, it is helpful to be aware of how scandalous it was for Jesus to even be having a conversation with this woman in the first place! But why?

First, Samaritans were in effect, a half-breed of their Jewish counterparts. Even though they shared the same ancestry, they were despised and not considered legitimate children of Israel.

Second, this woman's brief encounter with Jesus exposed that she had a horrible reputation in her community. There was no reason for Jesus to pay her any mind. But He does. Pause to meditate a moment on what this says about Jesus. Because of this exchange with someone otherwise easily passed over, we gain tremendous insight into the kind of true worshippers for whom God is searching.

Most compellingly, Christ declared His authority by comparing Himself to Jacob (the father and founder of the nation of Israel). Jesus illustrated this by contrasting the water that filled "Jacob's Well" with Himself and what He had to offer humanity. This historical well had existed for centuries, yet Jesus claimed Himself to be the personification of the "Living Well" whose unquenchable "water" had existed before the foundation of the world.

He was demonstrating that genuine worship would soon not be restricted to a mere physical building made by human hands. Rather, God would be accessible to all, wherever they might find themselves.

Christ then emphasizes a second time how important a concept this is to grasp:

> **God is Spirit, and those who worship Him must worship in spirit and truth.**
> **John 4:24 NKJV**

Jesus reveals that true worship can only come by means of the Holy Spirit. This is because God Himself is Spirit. Christ was also prophesying that anyone who was willing could, in fact, become a "housing" for His Spirit. God would soon reside in the very hearts of humanity through the authentic invitation from any individual. May we never take this beautiful promise so lightly!

This prophecy saw its initial fulfillment in the first chapters of the book of Acts and still exists as a free choice for every human even to this day!

Just "who" is this Spirit that provides access to worship God in spirit and in truth? How does it all work in conjunction with the accomplishment of salvation that Christ purchased for us on the cross?

The Helper is the Spirit of Truth, whom the world cannot receive, because it does not see Him or know Him; but you know Him because He remains with you and will be in you.

I will not leave you as orphans; I am coming to you.
John 14:17-18 NASB

What a phenomenal promise! Jesus said that He personally would send us a Helper. One that would guide us, lead us, warn us and encourage us. The caveat is that if you haven't first repented and accepted the Son's sacrifice for your sins, you will not be permitted to enjoy the counsel and empowerment of the Holy Spirit.

God will not share room in a heart that is not first and foremost submitted to Him.

Isn't it interesting how often the world doesn't seem to really get *who* Jesus is or *what* He's done or *why* it even matters? Though, it shouldn't come as a shock. One will never truly understand something that one first willingly rejects.

Once again, we can feel Jesus' very heart. He will not leave empty those who want to live for Him. God has promised that He "will not leave you nor forsake you." (See Deuteronomy 31:6-8.) This assurance should give us courage, even in the most desperate of times.

And we ought to give thanks to God always for you... that God chose you from the beginning to salvation, in sanctification of the Spirit, and belief of the truth, to which He called you.
2 Thessalonians 2:13-14 LSV

It is a marvelous truth to discover that as you chose God, you were also chosen by God. There are volumes upon volumes of writings, spanning centuries prior to our own, that have dealt with the breadth and depth of all this could possibly mean.

For our purposes in this chapter, what one should take away is a profound, unadulterated and eternal gratitude.

You have been called. You are chosen.

Those who are in Christ are being sanctified by the Spirit, and this happens because you've believed the truth. So rejoice! Because the deeper that you accept this, the more the stage is being set for throne-room entering and earth-shaking worship.

God wants to show Himself mighty in your life.

△△△

1. My TAKE AWAY from this chapter is...

2. This chapter makes me GRATEFUL because...

3. I will TAKE ACTION for this by...

1.11 | DENY YOURSELF

If anyone would come after Me, let him deny himself and take up his cross daily and follow Me.

Luke 9:23 ESV

In one of the most action-packed chapters in Luke's gospel, we read several rapid-fire accounts of Jesus' ministry. Many of which include Jesus sending out his disciples on a mission. Feeding the five thousand. Peter's confession of who Jesus really is. Being transfigured on the mountain. Jesus predicting His death (just to name a few.) Sandwiched in and among all these is Christ's command to "Deny Yourself."

Out of all the commands that could be asked of us, this has to be at the apex of difficulty when consistently attempting to put into practice. Why is this?

Probably because quite often, we love ourselves too much. Another way of saying it is that we are just *self*-ish.

It also shouldn't be a surprise (and it certainly does not help) that we live in one of the most self-focused generations the world has ever seen. From self-care to self-love to self-made, there is a seeming endless list of terms, books and instructional videos that begin and end with the *self*. While these terms could easily have a healthy application when exercised in moderation, they have instead become corrupted to the point where we lack the *self*-awareness to know when it crosses a border into toxicity.

Ironically we think the answer is within ourselves, when upon honest evaluation, we are quite easily deceived by ourselves.

Look at this example of Jesus' correcting Peter.

> **But turning around and seeing His disciples, He rebuked Peter and said, "Get behind Me, Satan; for you are not setting your mind on God's purposes, but on man's."**
>
> **And He... said to them, "If anyone wants to come after Me, he must deny himself, take up his cross, and follow Me."**
> **Mark 8:33-34 NASB**

Anytime we put our agenda before God's, we are thinking in terms that are anti-christ and, in fact, satanic in origin. The end results are often catastrophic and devastating.

Alongside denying oneself is a hard teaching with which to wrestle, but we see clear precedent above in Jesus' exchange with Peter. Remember that it was Satan (Lucifer) putting his agenda before God's that got him kicked out of Heaven. Subsequently, this is also the thinking that got Adam and Eve expelled from the garden.

We are told in Scripture elsewhere that "...just as the heavens are higher than the earth, so My ways are higher than your ways and My thoughts higher than your thoughts." (See Isaiah 55:9.) When hard times become difficult to understand, we must trust Jesus and set our mind on His ultimate purposes.

Self-denial isn't so much about the total loss of autonomy as it is the conscious declaration as to who has the ultimate authority over your life.

It's your choice. And the choice you make has drastically divergent destinations as we see in these next verses:

> **Therefore everyone who confesses Me before**

men, I will also confess him before My Father in Heaven.

But whoever denies Me before men, I will also deny him before My Father in Heaven.
Matthew 10:32-33 BSB

Again, we see this passage containing some very difficult truths. Ones with which, we must come to terms. That being said, you can also be certain that God is not looking for a reason to kick you out of Heaven or punish you. He's not on His throne in Heaven with lightning bolts ready to hurl down at you every time you make a mistake.

Rather, and as to not override our free will, God simply reciprocates our acceptance or denial of Him.

We must remember that Jesus died for each one of us, so we owe Him what's referred to as a "blood debt." This holds true for this existence, as well as for eternity. It is because of the blood guilt that we've heaped upon ourselves every time we've sinned. The consequences of our sins are eternal and this is why the solution —Christ's death—could be the only capital worthy of covering the infinite cost.

As we will study Jesus' command to "follow me" in our next chapter, we must first see the prerequisite to "deny yourself." Jesus is recorded saying elsewhere in the gospel of Matthew:

If anyone would come after Me, let him deny himself and take up his cross and follow Me.

For whoever would save his life will lose it, but whoever loses his life for My sake will find it.
Matthew 16:24-25 ESV

As you continue to develop the skill to command the joy that only Jesus can bring, understand that the solution is inside the equation of His commands. What does that mean?

We lose out on experiencing our ultimate significance when we live only for our own sake, our own agenda, and our own self.

The discipline of embracing Christ's authority over your life is the key to how you "deny yourself." The more we practice this, the more awareness we have of His Divine Presence in our lives. Just as true, the more we get this right, the more we will understand His will and calling for our lives. You want more insight?

Give more of your *self* to God.

ΔΔΔ

1. My TAKE AWAY from this chapter is...

2. This chapter makes me GRATEFUL because...

3. I will TAKE ACTION for this by...

1.12 | FOLLOW ME

**If anyone serves Me, let him follow Me; and where
I am, there My servant will be also. If anyone
serves Me, him My Father will honor.**
John 12:26 NKJV

Having just fulfilled prophecy (see Zechariah 9:9-13) in what is
referred to as the "triumphal entry," we join in on the scene
where a curious group of Greeks are seeing if Philip could get
them an audience with Jesus. Venturing out from an area that
has come to be known as the birthplace of modern philosophy,
they were intrigued by this increasingly popular Rabbi of the
Jews.

One can almost pick up an audible sigh from Jesus at this
request. At this point, He is laser-focused on completing the
mission that has now been set in motion by recent actions.

It is at this moment that He drops this incredibly unambiguous
command for all who are close around to hear. He even declares
that the God of Israel will honor them personally by their
agreement to the terms He just set. There can be no mistake
made here. Jesus is claiming to be the singular means for being
granted divine access to the Father!

His own disciples and followers hadn't quite yet understood the
full scope of where Jesus' ambitions were headed. He was days
away from the cross. To some in that very same crowd, He knew
it would soon mean their deaths in the months and years to
follow. Sadly, still to this day, there are many in this world that

follow Christ upon pain of death.

This notion is quite convicting for those of us who live in regions where—at least at this point in history—the worst we endure is being mocked or ridiculed for our faith. Still, for others who are faint of heart, consider the excuses sometimes given:

> **Jesus said to another, "Follow me." But he replied, "Lord, first let me go and..."**
> **Luke 9:59 NET**

How often have we allowed something or someone to get in the way of our following Christ? By the way, this is what's referred to as an "idol." To be clear, anything else that we prioritize before our faith journey with Christ has, in effect, become our god. This is not to say that we should neglect our families and friends or our work and commerce.

We should however, position our relationship with God at the pinnacle of our life experience and life rhythms.

Oftentimes just as damaging, we can get lured into the "comparison trap" as we follow Christ. We see this error in none other than Peter as he shares concern over his peer's (John's) future:

> **Jesus told him, "Keep following me."**
>
> **Peter turned around and noticed the disciple... (and) said, "Lord, what about him (John)?"**
>
> **Jesus told him... "How does that concern you? You must keep following Me!"**
> **John 21:19-22 ISV**

How often do you get tripped up by focusing too much at what's happening in the lives of others who are following Jesus?

Just as an Olympic athlete loses time off her stride whenever she looks in the next lane, we can experience similar setbacks when we're not concentrating on the finish line to which God has uniquely called us.

We must not be tempted to question why others enjoy blessings or advancement while we still seem to be in the same place. This can quickly devolve into bitterness and jealousy if we are not careful.

When our eyes are fixed on others, they are not focused on Jesus. Trust that God has a tailor-made process by which He refines you as an individual.

In this incredibly noisy world we live in, have you ever attempted to tune out all the other voices competing for your attention? Listen to this fantastic promise that Jesus offers those who follow Him:

> **My sheep listen to My voice, and I know them, and they follow Me; and I give them eternal life, and they will never perish; and no one will snatch them out of My hand.**
> **John 10:27-28 NASB**

It takes deliberate practice to enter into the quiet place with God.

Oh but when we do, the results are utterly remarkable and His Presence is so wonderful! God will only lead you as closely as you are willing to follow. The voice of God is accessible through His Word, as well as in prayer and devotion to Him. God is the "friend that sticks closer than a brother." (See Proverbs 18:24.)

Jesus gives one of the most comforting promises to those who take on this challenge to follow Him. He tells us that no one will be able to "snatch us out of His Hand."

God never drops the ball and He won't drop you as you learn to follow Him.

△△△

1. My TAKE AWAY from this chapter is…

2. This chapter makes me GRATEFUL because…

3. I will TAKE ACTION for this by…

JOY IN SURRENDER TO GOD

But let all those that put their trust in thee rejoice:
let them ever shout for joy, because thou
defendest them: let them also that love thy Name
be joyful in thee.

Psalm 5:11 KJV

2.1 | TAKE MY YOKE AND LEARN

Come to Me, all who labor and are heavy laden, and I will give you rest.

Take My yoke upon you, **and** learn from Me, **for I am gentle and lowly in heart, and you will find rest for your souls.**

For My yoke is easy, and My burden is light.
Matthew 11:28-30 ESV

This passage, at first glance, can seem counterintuitive because Jesus is saying that He will provide a rest and then asks us to carry a burden (or yoke).

In addition, He's not only asking us to carry a burden, but He's asking that we carry His burden. In our minds, there is no greater weight than the one that Christ held up on the cross.

Most Christians often experience a challenge with this passage due to a lack of proper context, setting and application. The scope of this command can seem daunting, yet it is important for us to grasp the actual word picture Jesus meant for us to see. Once we do, it invokes a sobering and fresh humility as we witness Christ's involvement in our daily lives.

Defined simply, a yoke was a "wooden bar placed over the neck of a pair of animals so they could pull together. Figuratively, it is what joins two people to move (or work) together as one."

So you see, it's not that Jesus is wanting to add one more thing to our already overflowing plates and overwhelming schedules. Rather, He is challenging us to throw aside the worldly burdens and world-views that often weigh down our minds and hearts, as well as our own thoughts and actions that accuse us daily. After this, we are invited to join with Him as we continue to move forward, together.

Deeper still, we also learn that the more experienced oxen are paired up with newer ones in order to "show them the ropes." The more seasoned ones set the pace, as well as shoulder the heavier portion of the burden, because it had become more familiar with the process.

Much in the same way, it is Christ encouraging us to move forward while at the same time, He is shouldering most of the load.

This is in stark contrast to the world and perhaps, the toxic people or situations that we've allowed in our lives in the past. These are things that ultimately hold us back. We are even warned about them in Scripture:

> Do not be unequally yoked **with unbelievers.
> For what partnership has righteousness with
> lawlessness? Or what fellowship has light with
> darkness?**
> **2 Corinthians 6:14 ESV**

Nor did Jesus mean for your faith journey to become cold, empty religious practice. Rather, He desires for you, a lifestyle invigorated by the power of the Holy Spirit:

> **Now, therefore,** why are you putting God to the test
> by placing a yoke **on the neck of the disciples
> that neither our fathers nor we have been able to**

bear?

But we believe that we will be saved through the grace of the Lord Jesus, just as they will.
Acts 15:10-11 ESV

Continuing the word picture from Christ's command, we are being openly invited again where He says, "learn from me."

It is an exhilarating and humbling experience to be in sync with the leading of the Holy Spirit in your life. The obvious follow up question here is, "Just how does one do this?" The Apostle Peter helps build confidence when he says this:

For to this you have been called, because Christ also suffered for you, leaving you an example, so that you might follow in His steps.
1 Peter 2:21 ESV

We learn from Jesus when we do what He's already told us to do (and what He's already done Himself.)

It was the psalmist who said, "Your Word have I hid in my heart that I might not sin against you." (See Psalm 119:11.) As we read and internalize Scripture, it begins to take root in our hearts. As we put into practice what we learn from the Bible, God begins to reveal Himself and His specific will over our lives.

Doing this also provides a type of peace and rest that Jesus promised when we obey. This is true mostly because we are simply doing what we were designed to do. When we are out of God's order, it weighs us down. However, learning from an omniscient God and being yoked alongside this same omnipotent Savior brings with it a joy and an encouragement, as well as a humble confidence that empowers us to live a life like no other.

$\triangle\triangle\triangle$

1. My TAKE AWAY from this chapter is...

2. This chapter makes me GRATEFUL because...

3. I will TAKE ACTION for this by...

2.2 | ABIDE IN ME

Abide in Me, and I in you. As the branch cannot bear fruit by itself, unless it abides in the vine, neither can you, unless you abide in Me.
John 15:4 ESV

Just imagine—for a moment—Jesus saying this, merely hours before He was to be betrayed, mocked, beaten and then led to be crucified!

Even with all this, Jesus' mind was on His disciples and by extension, you and me. His closest companions did not understand the severity of the moment and the lurking, imminent danger lying in wait. With no one else as a distraction, they were simply enjoying a well-earned, intimate meal together with their Rabbi and mentor. Little did they know that it would be their last before the unthinkable was to happen.

And it was in these ominous moments that Jesus spoke His clearest commands to His followers. It is right here that He presents one of the most sobering word-pictures. Essentially pointing to the difference between life or death, being purpose-filled or being purposeless.

He simply says, "Abide in Me."

Going even further, in order to better draw an even clearer line of distinction, He continues:

I am the vine; you are the branches. Whoever abides in Me and I in him, he it is that bears much fruit,

for apart from Me you can do nothing.

If anyone does not abide in Me he is thrown away like a branch and withers; and the branches are gathered, thrown into the fire, and burned.
John 15:5-6 ESV

On the one hand, Christ crystalizes the fact that if anyone wants a life of ultimate meaning, it would come only through true relationship with Him. If someone wants a fruitful life, it comes by being attached and engrafted into the will of God. He wants to multiply your capacity and ability, not limit it.

And on the other hand, willingly pulling away or saying no to the nourishment of the Holy Spirit to your soul can only lead to one place logically: Death.

One can serve no ultimate value when one does not value the Ultimate. Fire either refines or it consumes.

The very word *abide* speaks to a "constant mindfulness of" in combination with a "remaining inside the context." This speaks to the epitome of a willing, loving, two-sided relationship.

We experience a life in alignment with our highest purpose when we live our lives in the overflow and outflow of communion with our Savior.

Furthermore, as we faithfully practice abiding in Christ, we gain exclusive access to benefits that not everyone gets to enjoy. The psalmist shares that these promises of safety, protection, peace and rest are the result of this type of relationship:

He who dwells in the shelter of the Most High will abide in the shadow of the Almighty.

I will say to the LORD, "You are my refuge and my fortress, my God, in whom I trust."

As we look back to John's gospel, we see Jesus go one step further in revealing the access granted to us when we abide in Him:

If you abide in Me, **and** My words abide in you, **ask whatever you wish, and it will be done for you.**

By this My Father is glorified, that you bear much fruit and so prove to be My disciples.
John 15:7-8 ESV

There's a stunning clarity in this conditional promise: Our love for God, for His Word and for His will over our lives is in direct proportion to our heart's desires being fulfilled. This is not describing mere wish-fulfillment.

It's a wild idea to wrap our minds around! We make God look good when we live our lives to their fullest expression of surrender to Him. It is in this place that we receive favor, blessing and joy. What we produce for Him, proves us to be His disciples.

Lastly, Jesus finishes this thought of abiding in Him by revealing access to the most sought after treasures of humanity for all time. These being His love and His joy which is unlimited, unparalleled and incomparable.

As the Father has loved Me, so have I loved you. Abide in my love.

If you keep my commandments, you will abide in my love, **just as I have kept my Father's commandments and** abide in His love.

These things I have spoken to you, that my joy may

be in you, and that your joy may be full.

John 15:9-11 ESV

△△△

1. My TAKE AWAY from this chapter is...

2. This chapter makes me GRATEFUL because...

3. I will TAKE ACTION for this by...

2.3 | REMEMBER ME

And He took bread, and when He had given thanks, He broke it and gave it to them, saying, "This is my body, which is given for you. Do this in remembrance of Me."

And likewise the cup after they had eaten, saying, "This cup that is poured out for you is the new covenant in my blood."
LUKE 22:19-20 ESV

When was the last time you spent some meaningful, uninterrupted, void-of-distractions time meditating on Christ's command to "remember" Him? This was and is no small thing He is asking of us. We are being challenged to memorialize our Savior's death.

Have you recently stopped or even paused to seriously and soberly consider what Jesus has done for you by offering His faultless, blameless life in exchange for yours?

This lesson that Christ taught his disciples—one of the very last that He would before His death—was revealing in the fact that He was the very embodiment of what the Passover meal was pointing towards. For a few thousand years leading up to this moment, Israel had held an annual celebration of their deliverance from slavery in Egypt. A simple reading of Exodus 12 confirms the many connections that are made between the original Passover and then, this "last supper" that preceded the cross.

Think about it:

The timeline of events themselves. The covering of wooden door posts with blood. The eating of unleavened bread (which symbolizes sinlessness). A meal meant to be eaten in haste, where you must be fully dressed to leave at a moment's notice. The complete and total pouring out of the blood of a spotless lamb.

All of these allusions and more, culminating in the final judgment of God's wrath upon the first born.

The writer of Hebrews explains that all this was meant to point to Jesus. He is the fulfillment of all prophecy, as He is both the ultimate offering and the perfect priest to offer it:

> **For since the law has but a shadow of the good things to come instead of the true form of these realities, it can never... make perfect those who draw near...**
>
> **But when** Christ had offered for all time a single sacrifice for sins, **He sat down at the right hand of God,**
> **HEBREWS 10:1, 12 ESV**

The claim towards Christ's supreme authority in the above Scripture speaks matter-of-factly when it depicts Christ as the "true form of these realities," as well as the completion of God's plan of salvation for all humankind. These are realities that present Jesus as the one *real* Savior. The one who became our *real* escape from a *real* Hell by making a *real* way for us into a *real* Heaven by becoming a *real* sacrifice for our *real* sins.

Yes. It is *really* that absolute.

This is one reason why today's ceremony and celebration of Communion is meant to be so tangible, so "touch-able." It is meant to call us back to a place where we engage our entire being as we participate. Our body, our mind and our spirit are called into harmony through this ceremony as we "proclaim the Lord's death until He comes."

Do this in remembrance of me.

For as often as you eat this bread and drink this cup, you proclaim the Lord's death until He comes...

Each one must examine himself before he eats of the bread and drinks of the cup.
1 CORINTHIANS 11:25-26, 28 ESV

We also learn from Paul's letter to the church at Corinth that we are to "examine ourselves beforehand." Why is this? Because we must authentically honor Christ's death when we celebrate the ceremony of Communion.

Have you ever seen someone be disrespectful at a funeral? It angers us and it should anger us. Especially if the one being eulogized gave their life for you and the person being disrespectful! Imagine how it grieves the heart of our Heavenly Father when we take the sacred memorial of His "one and only Son" half-heartedly. Let all of yourself be genuinely present in these opportunities.

Lastly, what is so touching about this expression of Christ's desire for His disciples to "Remember Me" is that He leads by the example of His own remembrance of us.

Consider Jesus' response to the thief on the cross next to Him as he cried out to Jesus, and only a few moments before Christ died Himself. This thief came to a humble awareness of his own sin and apparently a revelation of Christ's sinlessness and supremacy as King.

A common thief came to grips with the gravity of this moment. How much more should we? In our own way, we are that thief.

Read the exchange below that he had with Jesus. See if you can identify with his heart's cry and find hope for yourself in Jesus' response:

> **And he said, "Jesus, remember me when you come into your kingdom."**
>
> **And He (Jesus) said to him, "Truly, I say to you, today you will be with me in paradise."**
> **LUKE 22:42-43 ESV**

We often ask Jesus to remember us in our needs. How often will you remember Him for what He's already done?

△△△

1. My TAKE AWAY from this chapter is...

2. This chapter makes me GRATEFUL because...

3. I will TAKE ACTION for this by...

2.4 | BE READY

You also must be ready, for the Son of Man is coming at an hour you do not expect.
LUKE 12:40 ESV

We live in a technology driven age where we can call or text any guests that we're expecting at any point. We can ask them how far away they are and when google says they'll be arriving. Even more astounding, they can share their journey from their Uber and we can watch their movement in real time.

Everything and everyone was not always so easily accessible. Life and living required far more patience.

Not too long ago, family and friends that would be visiting from far away could only give a rough estimate of when they might arrive. There would be so much excitement as we made our homes and ourselves presentable, while also preparing a meal for their arrival. A little nerve-racking and fun, all at the same time. You just weren't completely sure when they would be arriving, so you wanted to be ready. Then, after what sometimes seemed like forever, you would suddenly see their vehicle pulling up outside your window.

That feeling! So much built up anxiety or uncertainty, all at once replaced by sheer joy (as well as a sigh of relief.) The wait was over! They are here.

A similar environment is the setting that Jesus uses in our passage for today. Let's take a look at the preceding verses to get a clear understanding of exactly what Jesus meant when He commands His disciples to "Be Ready."

> Stay dressed for action **and** keep your lamps
> burning...
> **LUKE 12:35 ESV**

The metaphors used by Jesus here are incredibly potent:

Stay dressed. One only needs to consult Ephesians 6:10-20 to get a complete understanding of what it means to be outfitted head-to-toe with the "armor of God."

For action. This armor is not for passive appearances only. Staying perpetually equipped is how warriors stay ready for active battle. This is true for those wars that are waged on the outside of us (where we're called to take a stand), as well as the war that rages within us.

Keep your lamps burning. Could there be any clearer picture of the need for the fires of our hearts to stay continually lit for God? This happens only through the access and acquiescence to the power of the Holy Spirit working inside of us. The passage continues:

> Be like men who are waiting **for their master to
> come home from the wedding feast, so that they
> may open the door to him at once when he comes
> and knocks.**
> **LUKE 12:36 ESV**

We can see the above Scripture being fulfilled, in addition to the blessing it brings us, in two senses:

First, preparing ourselves to "be ready" points to the ultimate promise of Jesus' coming back to receive us into His Kingdom.

Second, when our preparation and awareness is raised in the

daily sense, we stay open and ready every time Jesus knocks on the door of our hearts to reveal Himself in some new and compelling way. This point is further explained by Jesus in the next verses.

> Blessed are those **servants whom the master** finds **awake when he comes. Truly, I say to you, he will dress himself for service and have them recline at the table, and he will come and serve them.**
>
> **If he...** finds them awake, blessed are those **servants!**
>
> LUKE 12:37-38 ESV

Now this is where it gets really interesting. Of course, we can clearly see that Jesus is coming for the express reason of blessing those who've been faithful waiting for Him.

Now, that being said, let's not gloss to quickly over the line that reads, "He [the Master, aka Jesus] will dress Himself for service and have them [the servants, aka, you and I] recline at the table, and He will come and serve them."

How incredible is this promise? Jesus returns our servitude with His own. He will not be outdone! This is one of the chief factors that distinguishes Christ from other false gods mentioned in other religions.

In Philippians 2:7, we are told that Jesus didn't only come to lord His authority over humanity "but [He] emptied Himself, by taking the form of a servant."

It may be that we thought that this was all about our expectation of His return. While that is certainly part of the equation, we learn here that His passion for welcoming us into His Heaven exponentially outweighs our own anticipation by comparison.

After saying all this, Jesus gives us one more shocking statement:

> **But know this, that** if the master of the house had known at what hour the thief was coming, **he would not have left his house to be broken into.**
>
> **LUKE 12:39 ESV**

And it's in this verse that we see Jesus "tipping His hand" in two more ways. Initially, He is speaking to matters we've already discussed. "That no man knows the day or the hour..." (See Matthew 24:36.)

However, He's also making an even more provocative claim. He is prophesying to his disciples that He is about to break into the stronghold of Death, Hell and the grave and take back the keys that belonged to Him!

So we see that readiness is a state of the mind, an obedience of the body and a posturing of the spirit. We end today where we began:

> **You also must be ready, for the Son of Man is coming at an hour you do not expect.**
>
> **LUKE 12:40 ESV**

ΔΔΔ

1. My TAKE AWAY from this chapter is...

2. This chapter makes me GRATEFUL because...

3. I will TAKE ACTION for this by...

2.5 | BE HUMBLE

The greatest among you shall be your servant.

Whoever exalts himself will be humbled, and
whoever humbles himself will be exalted.
MATTHEW 23:11-12 ESV

Let's first set this scene properly.

Why? Because this is too good an opportunity to pass up, as it was an incredibly heated and intense exchange with many onlookers!

It's also quite comical as Jesus had been getting grilled all day by the religious leaders of that community. (See Matt 22.) They were trying to catch Him in a contradiction over various matters regarding taxes, the law, and the resurrection.

Every baited question had a "catch-22" built into its premise in order to trap Jesus. All while in front of His disciples and followers, no less! And, in true Messiah-like fashion, Jesus not only navigates this mine field of brutal cross-examination flawlessly, but He even exposes the hypocrisy of both His skeptics and the cynics.

Jesus then uses this teachable moment in front of the crowd, His disciples, as well as His opposition to call out pride for what it was. Sin. He then calls everyone towards the higher (and harder) way of humility.

All throughout recorded history it is often noted that those who have power, authority and influence over others, have used it in a way that subjects others to their rule. Many times this has happened in some deeply disturbing and tragic ways.

Flipping this centuries-long narrative of domination on its head, Christ made it clear to all the crowd that it would not work this way among His followers.

Those who wanted be seen as the *greatest* in His Kingdom would have to present themselves as a *servant* to all.

It is fantastically counter-intuitive to think that being humble would grant any opportunity for the "leveling up" of one's life. However, that is exactly what Scripture teaches us:

> **Clothe yourselves, all of you, with humility toward one another, for "God opposes the proud but gives grace to the humble."**
>
> **Humble yourselves, therefore, under the mighty hand of God so that at the proper time He may exalt you, casting all your anxieties on Him, because He cares for you.**
>
> **1 PETER 5:5-7 ESV**

Consider Peter's words in the above passage. Humility becomes another item of apparel with which we are to clothe ourselves. Thus becoming a metaphor for how we are to project ourselves outwardly to others with a Christ-like attitude. Just as someone could easily see us wearing say, a blue shirt, as we walk past them, they should also be able to recognize our humility in the way we carry ourselves and interact with them.

Peter also speaks to the fact that pride gets on God's last nerve! God actively postures Himself against those who are prideful. He hates this kind of arrogance and is unwilling to even give it a hearing.

Lastly, in the above passage, this "if/then" type promise of being exalted is actually rooted in as well as the result of time. Faithful humility is the litmus test God uses to raise us up and prepare us for great influence.

Our Heavenly Father, in fact, is actively seeking for those who are humble:

> **...But this is the one to whom I will look: he who is humble and contrite in spirit and trembles at My Word.**
> **ISAIAH 66:2 ESV**

Whenever we minimize the sin in our lives or whenever trivialize His Word spoken over our lives, we create a problem for our lives. This problem is what God calls pride.

He is on the lookout for people with repentant hearts, as well as those who highly value Scripture. He holds this type of follower very dear to Himself.

When you take His Word seriously, He'll take your words (i.e. your prayers) seriously. Listen to this interaction between God and the prophet Daniel:

> **Then He (God) said to me, "Fear not, Daniel, for from the first day that you set your heart to understand and humbled yourself before your God, your words have been heard, and I have come because of your words..."**
> **DANIEL 10:12 ESV**

Just this notion alone that God listens more intently to those who will simply be humble should be enough motivation for us all to grow in this area. Daniel's heart for being humble towards

God also reveals another secret:

Humility brings us to a place where every fear dissipates and where wisdom flourishes in our lives.

Ironically enough, God often ignores the loud, obnoxious, showy, pretentious shows of pride. At the same time, it seems that humility is the megaphone that will get God's attention every time.

ΔΔΔ

1. My TAKE AWAY from this chapter is...

2. This chapter makes me GRATEFUL because...

3. I will TAKE ACTION for this by...

2.6 | BE PERFECT

You therefore must be perfect, as your Heavenly Father is perfect.
Matthew 5:48 ESV

I know. I get it. The most obvious of all questions follows a command like this:

"How can anyone be *perfect*?!?!"

Especially in comparison to God? On the surface, this is preposterous. In and of ourselves, perfection would be unquestionably unattainable.

So why the command to "be perfect," knowing that we would fail? Was Jesus trying to purposely humiliate us mere humans with such an outlandish expectation or is there something we are missing to better understand His intentions here? More context will certainly help us.

Referred to as the "Sermon on the Mount," we see Jesus addressing a large group of people, as well as a multitude of issues (many of which we'll discuss in other chapters.) Jesus gives us a quick, bullet point proclamation of the type of lifestyle that honors and pleases God. Some are spoken with an instruction designed as a warning, while others come with a blessing attached for those who rise to its challenge.

Then, it is here in verse 48 where we are given the sum total to all of these teaching points: "Be Perfect."

Perfection, as a term itself, has tragically suffered the same fate as many otherwise attention-getting words of our day. Sadly it has become a toxic term for at least two reasons.

One, it's become overused and therefore has lost most of its value when being spoken.

Even more disappointing, the term has slowly become disconnected from God and His Holiness altogether. The *comparison trap* of perfection has little to do anymore with the conviction of sin and falling short of God's glory. In only a couple of generations, it has now devolved to describe the way we denigrate ourselves in comparison with others who seem to be doing better than we are in life.

So the redemption of this word rests in the biblical worldview in which it is meant to be understood. Look at what James, the half-brother of Jesus has to say:

For you know that the testing of your faith produces steadfastness.

And let steadfastness have its full effect, that you may be perfect and complete, lacking in nothing.
James 1:3-4 ESV

What is being described above by James is important for us to grasp in order to clearly understand Jesus' command. The *HELPS Word Studies* unpacks this even more: to "be perfect" is to be "mature from going through the necessary stages to reach the end-goal, i.e. developed into a consummating completion by fulfilling the necessary process (spiritual journey.)"

Meaning that the goal is a life-long, healthy and intentional pursuit of being a mature Christian. It's about completing the unique journey that God gave you, while also embracing His process that brings wholeness to your life.

However, James mentions only one side of the coin in this verse.

There's still the looming and intimidating qualifier of Jesus' command to "be perfect."

He added God's perfection as as the metric when He says, "Be perfect, [even] as your Heavenly Father is perfect." If you're thinking that this isn't possible, you're right.

That's the point. And this point is made to point you straight to Jesus.

> **Although He (Jesus) was a son, He learned obedience through what He suffered.**
>
> **And being made perfect, He became the source of eternal salvation to all who obey Him...**
> **Hebrews 5:8-9 ESV**

Again, James tackles the part of the equation that is handed to us as a challenge to pursue perfection through process. Thankfully, the writer of Hebrews provides a sigh of relief to remind us that it is only in Jesus' sacrifice on the cross that we can truly be seen as perfect. Here's how it works:

Christ alone was and is perfect. We receive His perfect sacrifice as covering for our sin. He then covers us with His perfection. Now, we are perfect in Him.

Paul understood this and in the next passage, he points us to the ultimate finish line of our promised perfection, when we are all called heavenward to experience eternity with Christ.

There awaits a euphoric fullness of total comprehension and intimate connection for us all who have put our faith in Jesus.

> **For we know in part and we prophesy in part, but when the perfect comes, the partial passes away.**
> **1 Corinthians 13:9-10 ESV**

This command of Christ was meant to call us to honest self-evaluation and examination before God. There is no denying that each of us have either missed the mark, crossed a line or fallen short of God's glory.

How encouraging it is that He continues to use imperfect, broken beings to speak of His perfect love and sacrifice for us!

Paul also provides us with a living hope that all our misguided misgivings are, for now, covered by Christ. Even more encouraging, we know that one day we will be utterly changed altogether from this failed existence to be truly perfect before our Heavenly Father forever.

△△△

1. My TAKE AWAY from this chapter is...

2. This chapter makes me GRATEFUL because...

3. I will TAKE ACTION for this by...

2.7 | DON'T BE A HYPOCRITE

Watch out! Don't do your good deeds publicly, to be admired by others, for you will lose the reward from your Father in Heaven... don't do as the hypocrites do.

Matthew 6:1-2 NLT

We all know *that* person.

The one who does something good, perhaps even from a benevolent place, but mostly just to be seen doing it.

From the propagandizing of political figures, to the rich and famous, who sometimes disgustingly posture themselves as an "advocate." Even normal, everyday people fall prey to hypocrisy as they seem to be desperately seeking likes, hearts, follows and affirmation from others to acknowledge their well doing on social media. Doesn't it just leave us all with a bad taste in our mouths? Like a rose set inside a pile of manure, sometimes you can almost smell the smokescreen.

However, if we're being honest, we've probably all done this at one time or another ourselves, haven't we?

To be fair, there is nothing wrong with being an advocate or using your influence and good works to raise awareness for a worthwhile cause. Scripture teaches elsewhere that we should do this. That being said, the context clues from our reading today shows us clearly that we're talking about something else altogether. We'll be examining our motives as well as our intended audience.

So, who are you trying to impress? That's the root Jesus was pulling at in His command to not be a hypocrite. He then shares three examples in addition to offering three antidotes. Let's look at the first of these:

> **When you give to someone in need,** don't do as the hypocrites do—**blowing trumpets in the synagogues and streets to call attention to their acts of charity! I tell you the truth, they have received all the reward they will ever get.**
>
> **But when you give to someone in need, don't let your left hand know what your right hand is doing.**
>
> **Matthew 6:2-3 NLT**

The first example above is in the area of giving. Think about the times when you see it blasted on the news or social media. We're talking about the obnoxiously big check being presented publicly. Be candid. Aren't we skeptically curious about the motives behind the gift almost every time?

Jesus is effectively saying, "Ok. Great. You already got your blessing by making a big scene when you gave it."

In stark contrast, have you ever heard about someone way after the fact (whether famous or not, corporation or individual) giving generously to some tragic situation or legitimate need? Maybe it was done behind-the-scenes and maybe it wasn't revealed until many months or even years afterwards.

Doesn't that instantly make you think more highly of that person or organization? Why is that? Because, more often than not, their secrecy made it clear that their motives were pure.

So we see Jesus' remedy as He says, "But when you give..."

He then explains how we can both enjoy the euphoria of generosity, while at the same time not dwelling on the desire for acknowledgement after it's done.

He then goes on to tackle the next trap of hypocrisy:

> **When you pray, don't be like the hypocrites who love to pray publicly on street corners and in the synagogues where everyone can see them. I tell you the truth, that is all the reward they will ever get.**
>
> **But when you pray, go away by yourself, shut the door behind you,**
> **Matthew 6:5-6 NLT**

This example is not about standing up for your faith in the public square. This has everything to do with not being arrogant and showy when you pray.

Elsewhere in the gospels, Jesus tells a parable of two men. (See Luke 18:9-14.) The first, a deeply religious man and the other, a man despised by most of society. The first prays loudly to God (and more accurately, so that the crowd around him could hear) about how important he was and all the good that he had done. He even started comparing his goodness with the wickedness of the second man.

This second man was acutely aware of his sinfulness (to the point where he beats his chest in travailing) when contrasted against the holiness of God.

Jesus gives the moral of the story quite pointedly when He says, "I tell you, this sinner, not the Pharisee, returned home justified before God." (See Luke 18:14.)

Whenever your worship or prayer distracts people's attention from God and onto you, check your motives.

Lastly, Jesus turns His attention to our motives when we fast:

> **And when you fast,** don't make it obvious, as the hypocrites do, **for they try to look miserable and disheveled so people will admire them for their fasting. I tell you the truth, that is the only reward they will ever get.**
>
> **But when you fast, comb your hair and wash your face.**
>
> **Then no one will notice that you are fasting, except your Father,**
> **Matthew 6:16-18 NLT**

Fasting is meant to be a truly composite test of the body, mind and spirit. To set aside for a time the satisfaction of a meal to be sustained instead by our love for and devotion to God.

Jesus is telling us not to miss out on our blessing by looking for other people's praise rather than God's. Again, this "but when you fast" approach reveals true motive. Create the habit of not whining about being hungry during these times. Also, try to look your best outwardly when you fast so that only God will know what you're doing.

We're familiar with the beautiful picture of a little child, eager for his parent's approval when showing them their latest work of art. In that same spirit, we should give, pray and fast in a way where the heart of our intentions is to get the attention of our Heavenly Father.

> Give your gifts... Pray... fast... in private **and your Father, who sees everything, will reward you.**
> **Matthew 6:4, 6, 18 NLT**

△△△

1. My TAKE AWAY from this chapter is...

2. This chapter makes me GRATEFUL because...

3. I will TAKE ACTION for this by...

2.8 | DON'T MAKE VOWS

**You have also heard that our ancestors were told,
"You must not break your vows; you must carry
out the vows you make to the Lord."**

But I say, "Do not make any vows!"
Matthew 5:33-34 NLT

We turn our attention once again to the Sermon on the Mount. This time, Jesus issues a command that almost seems to go against what we would otherwise see as a noble and righteous practice—that of making vows to God or to others.

Why is it that Jesus would not only warn us against making vows, but go even further by commanding us not to do so?

There is a whole list of narratives throughout the history of Scripture where we see vows being spoken among tribes and nations from man to man, man to God and even God to man.

So why the seeming "about face" on the matter?

A quick study of the many man-made vows throughout the thousands of years of biblical record reveal a disappointing truth. It was from this fundamental fact that Jesus was speaking:

We (the human race) at best have a terrible track record of keeping our promises, and at worst, making really dumb ones.

King Solomon in Ecclesiastes gives us a glimpse into this when he shares this:

> **It is better not to vow than to make a vow and not fulfill it.**
>
> **Do not let your mouth cause your flesh to sin, and do not tell the messenger that your vow was a mistake. Why should God be angry with your words and destroy the work of your hands?**
> **Ecclesiastes 5:5-6 NLT**

Solomon's teaching cuts right to the marrow of the folly of making vows.

Have you ever made a solemn vow (or promise or commitment) and broke it? How embarrassing and how much shame did you feel as a result? Did it hurt the relationship or shake your integrity? Maybe you were the one on the receiving end of the promise made? Where someone conveniently changed what the agreement actually was from the beginning. How'd that feel? It might have even become the tipping point that caused you to severe ties with them completely. At the least, it should have caused you to "get it in writing" next time.

Now, lay those thoughts alongside the more fearful possibility that Solomon gives us by warning that God might actually allow something we put our energy into, to become destroyed because of our foolish words.

God not only listens to our commitments we make with Him, He also listens to our promises made with other people!

Can you imagine how annoyed God is when, as a part of your vow, you add qualifiers that you have no power over? Listen to Jesus make this point:

> **And do not say, "By the earth!" because the earth is**

82

His footstool.

And do not say, "By Jerusalem!" **for Jerusalem is the city of the great King.**

Do not even say, "By my head!" **for you can't turn one hair white or black.**
Matthew 5: 35-36 NLT

Think about it! How often do we make promises while adding phrases that are not quantifiable or speaking to things that we even have no authority over? Foolish declarations like, "on my mother's grave" or "on my kid's life." (A despicable vow just like this is tragically described in Judges 11:30-40.)

People often say such things to make themselves seem more serious or sincere. However, think about the times you've heard vows like these mentioned above. The person almost loses instant credit with their hearers because they're attempting to offer up something as collateral that couldn't or shouldn't be collected upon, regardless of their follow through (or not).

James helps us simplify our lives by teaching us that a simple "yes" or "no" will do for those who live their lives with integrity:

But most of all, my brothers and sisters, never take an oath, **by heaven or earth or anything else. Just** say a simple yes or no, **so that you will not sin and be condemned.**
James 5:12 NLT

It is for the sake of avoiding temptation from the evil one (see Matthew 5:37), as well as being condemned or humiliated that we need to be mindful about how we make our commitments.

This last point made by both Jesus and James is key to

understand. The enemy is always lying in wait to trap us by our own foolishly spoken words. He stands brazenly, always ready to accuse us before God. So, don't give him the opportunity!

By most counts, one of the most sought after types of relationships are those who will simply say "yes" or "no" and then fulfill their word.

One life's best principles: Underpromise, then overdeliver.

You don't need to convince anyone of how serious you are because your follow through has done the heavy lifting of building trust.

As the saying goes, "actions speak louder than words."

ΔΔΔ

1. My TAKE AWAY from this chapter is...

2. This chapter makes me GRATEFUL because...

3. I will TAKE ACTION for this by...

2.9 | DON'T BE ANXIOUS

And He said to His disciples, "Therefore I tell you, do not be anxious about your life, **what you will eat, nor about your body, what you will put on.**

And which of you by being anxious **can add a single hour to his span of life?**

If then you are not able to do as small a thing as that, why are you anxious **about the rest?"**
Luke 12:22, 25-26 ESV

Remarkably, this particular instruction from Christ is sandwiched between two teachings on money. While many of us may have an inclination to worry for any number of reasons, Jesus calls out an unmistakable and specific correlation between our finances and our anxieties.

God, robed in the flesh, also understood all too well the temptation of greed that spikes up ever-so-quickly inside the human psyche. He has been watching this vicious cycle play out within humanity ever since He created us.

We constantly worry about what we don't have. In similarly striking fashion, we panic about the possibility of losing whatever we may have gained.

The problem is, we're always wanting more and this is what causes a large majority of our anxiety and worries in life.

How fascinating that Jesus uses the illustration of our inability to use "worry" as a means for adding time to our life. In fact, it does quite the opposite. While common knowledge now, it was a relatively short time ago that the medical community learned that anxiety can actually shorten our lifespan.

Important to note however, is that there is certainly a distinction between panic and careful planning. God is not against us being intentional with the planning process. (Jesus speaks to this elsewhere. See Luke 14:25-33.) What we have in this command is an opportunity to see how the "tests" we encounter in life reveal areas where we trust God, as well as where we have room to grow. The psalmist explains:

Search me, O God, and know my heart; test me and
know my anxious thoughts.

Point out anything in me that offends you, and lead
me along the path of everlasting life.
Psalm 139:23-24

Can you legitimately say this same prayer to God in the case of your own heart and mind? Inside this simple prayer is a formula that is so humble and so honest. The psalmist's heart is that God would search, test, know, point out and lead him to a better way of living.

Life is often a trial by fire, as is our faith in God.

Our life experiences (the good and bad) are where our emotions and thought life are put to the test. And, it is in these very moments, we are called to "take every thought captive" that offends Christ. Thus, when successful, we can continue to move forward confidently in the path of life that has been marked out for us by the will of God.

Our thoughts and our emotions are lenses into the level of faith that we exercise towards God. In the next few verses, we pick up on the initial teaching by Jesus:

> **He will certainly care for you. Why do you have such little faith?**
>
> **...Don't worry about such things.**
>
> **These things dominate the thoughts of unbelievers all over the world, but your Father already knows your needs.**
> **Luke 12:29-30 NLT**

How different would our lives be if we could just pause before a moment of panic and simply pray with this teaching in mind? Faith-filled prayer changes everything when we let our hearts cry out in the midst of our trials.

God is completely aware of how you're feeling and what you need right now. Trust the calming power of the Holy Spirit in moments of anxiety.

When these worldly thoughts dominate our lives—as Jesus mentions—He calls it out as greed and as a lack of faith. This is not to say that we are to be lazy or idle in the stead of anxiety either. Scripture warns against this just as fiercely. We are called to be active in our participation of the desired result.

It's been said by many a preacher, "You do what you can do in the natural and God will add His *super*natural." That's a powerful combination!

After doing this, we can trust God with the results as the Apostle Peter encourages us:

> **Casting all your anxieties on Him, because He cares for you.**
> **1 Peter 5:7 ESV**

How fantastic a statement and promise this is! God loves you. He cares for you. So much so, that He is willing to bear the burden of not only your sin, but also your anxieties and worries.

The decision is yours: Hold on to your anxiety or releasing it to the hands of God?

Holding brings harm. Releasing brings relief.

ΔΔΔ

1. My TAKE AWAY from this chapter is...

2. This chapter makes me GRATEFUL because...

3. I will TAKE ACTION for this by...

2.10 | WALK IN THE LIGHT

Jesus replied, "My light will shine for you just a little longer. Walk in the light while you can, **so the darkness will not overtake you. Those who walk in the darkness cannot see where they are going."**
John 12:35 NLT

Here, we enter the town of Jerusalem, mere days away from Jesus' crucifixion. He had just fulfilled the centuries old prophecy of the "triumphal entry" and the crowds were awestruck.

Philip and Andrew, who were Jesus' disciples, had just received a request from a group of Greeks that were curious about meeting their Rabbi.

A most startling bit of irony arises out of this scene. Despite all Jesus was doing and the people's fascination with Him, many still would not believe in Him as the promised Messiah. This is where we read above of Christ's warning to his opposers, as well as His command to His followers to "walk in the Light."

Jesus was saying something quite strange to His hearers in predicting His death. It was believed and accepted by the Jews that the Messiah would be incapable of death. Hindsight being twenty-twenty, it is now clearly understood that the Messiah was meant to conquer death, through His death and the power of His resurrection.

Much like the crowd back then, we are all commanded to walk in the light of our Savior. Jesus had additionally mentioned this truth only a chapter beforehand. Here we're given an illustration that we've all most likely experienced before:

> **If anyone** walks in the day, he does not stumble, **because** he sees the light **of this world.**
>
> **But if anyone** walks in the night, he stumbles, **because the** light is not in him.
> **John 11:9-10 ESV**

So, there's that moment in the middle of the night. You know the one. When you're still half asleep but need go to the restroom. Walking around with nothing more on your mind other than getting back to your bed and then...pain. Searing pain. You've stubbed your toe or stepped on something you didn't even know was there. Now you're awake, confused and probably pretty perturbed.

Now play that same scenario out, but this time, in the matter of your soul.

Jesus wants us to walk in His Light because He knows that when we don't, we stumble. We hurt ourselves. We know this to be true as well. Nevertheless, we are still tempted towards spiritual slumber and darkness. Our Heavenly Father loves us and does not wish for our pain. He wants us to see clearly through the light that only He can provide.

The Apostle John wrote a few other letters in addition to his account of the gospel. It's here where he leans into this concept. Causing us to examine our hearts a little bit more intently:

> **If we say we have fellowship with Him while** we walk in darkness, we lie **and do not practice the**

truth.

But if we walk in the light, as He is in the light, we have fellowship **with one another, and the blood of Jesus his Son cleanses us from all sin.**
1 John 1:6-7 ESV

What do you practice? The word *practice* is so vital to this teaching. What do your daily and weekly routines reveal about you?

As Christians, we carry a license to practice our faith as we follow Jesus. This is actually what unites us all together. One of the demarcations of a disciple is the community we all share together. It is where we encourage and hold each other accountable to practice our walk.

We have the ability to do this both with reverence and without shame because of Jesus' perfect sacrifice for our sins. Genuine joy and happiness are both wrapped tightly in this truth, as the Psalmist so eloquently tells us:

Happy are those who hear the joyful call to worship, for they will walk in the light of your presence, **LORD.**

They rejoice all day long in your wonderful reputation. They exult in your righteousness.
Psalm 89:15-16 NLT

This passage really presents some exciting and inspiring questions for those who will take up the challenge to walk in His Light.

How is your "joy meter" affected when you engage in worship? When was the last time you made worship about how you want to make God feel, rather than yourself?

Again, the Psalmist paints such beautiful scene. Have you ever been in a moment of worship, prayer or reading Scripture when, all of a sudden, everything just becomes clearer? It's almost like Heaven is beaming down on you with a thousand-watt flood light on your soul! There is something so illuminating about walking in the Presence of God. The Holy Spirit has an excellent reputation for this kind of experience in the life of the believer.

Jesus loves to shine down on you (and in you) as you walk in His Light.

ΔΔΔ

1. My TAKE AWAY from this chapter is...

2. This chapter makes me GRATEFUL because...

3. I will TAKE ACTION for this by...

2.11 | WATCH AND PRAY

Watch and pray that you may not enter into temptation. The spirit indeed is willing, but the flesh is weak.
Mark 14:38 ESV

Even at the darkest hours of Jesus' time here on earth, His heart was steadfast in mentoring his disciples.

The passage above is set inside the famous Garden of Gethsemane where Jesus betrayal is imminent. Knowing the gut-wrenching scene that was about to take place, He had stepped away for some alone time with His Father to be restrengthened in His resolve. Can you imagine His disappointment to come back and see His most trusted followers in a deep sleep? It was at this moment, right before being betrayed by Judas, that Jesus teaches them this command that we see Mark reporting in his gospel.

The intersection of where these individual commands meet (to watch and pray) are vitally essential in the life of the disciple. Many important studies can be (and have been) made of each word. However, for our reflection today, we must simply grasp and apply how they work together.

There is an inescapable expectation on Christ's part for us to be vigilant, acutely aware and engaged against the enemy, as well as our own weaknesses. We are to subdue our own body, mind and spirit under subjection to the Holy Spirit. Inside of each one of us, we must crave to listen and act upon the spiritual calling from God at a higher decibel than our own fleshly desires.

While we should be at peace because God is greater than any challenge we might encounter, we are also on high alert against the enemy. In Israel's history, the leader Nehemiah mentions this brilliant strategy:

All of them (the enemy) conspired together to come and attack... and create confusion.

Nevertheless we made our prayer **to our God, and because of them** we set a watch **against them day and night.**
Nehemiah 4:8-9 NKJV

Perhaps one helpful metaphor to understand what it means to watch in Scripture is to see it in the context of "working a shift." It's a block of time set aside in order to devote special attention to perform specific responsibilities.

Nehemiah knew the threats of the enemy were all too real and could only be outmatched by a strategic counter on Israel's part. The following plan was ceaselessly managed by Nehemiah as groups of men rotated in and out of taking shifts of being on high alert as well as others who would continue the work on building the wall. The results speak for themselves. (See Nehemiah, chapter 4.)

Much in the same way, we must set aside blocks of time throughout our days and weeks to engage in spiritual warfare against the enemy. And not merely for our own selves! This is where the power of a group of trusted friends and family can come together. Even when we're all apart physically, we still can all be lifting each other up prayerfully at different "watches" throughout the day and night.

There is yet another way we see the union of our watching and our praying coming together in a most thrilling way. When we pray to God in expectancy and hope:

Listen to my words, LORD, Consider my sighing.

Listen to the sound of my cry for help, my King and my God, For to You I pray.

In the morning, LORD, You will hear my voice; In the morning I will present my prayer to You and be on the watch.

Psalm 5:1-3 NASB

We read here, not only the lines of the Psalmist above, but it also seems we can read-between-the-lines as he uses expressions of despair and exhaustion.

He speaks of "sighing" and his "cry for help." Two wells of emotions we've all drawn from at times. Then, we see something else quite surprising. You can feel the sense of expectation as he is up early in the morning to see God work mightily on his behalf.

When was the last time you prepared yourself, truly believing and waiting for your miracle to be manifested?

As mentioned before, many in the modern military still understand the principles spoken in this command. It is a lifestyle for them. Paul knew this and keyed in on it in his letter to the church at Ephesus:

And take the helmet of salvation, and the Sword of the Spirit, which is the Word of God; praying always with all prayer **and supplication in the Spirit,** being watchful **to this end with all perseverance and supplication for all the saints —and for me, that utterance may be given to me,**

**that I may open my mouth boldly to make known
the mystery of the gospel,**
Ephesians 6:17-19 NKJV

Being watchful and being prayerful are individually, powerful practices. However, when they are combined, the result is exponential.

May we all learn to marry these two together and see God at work on our behalf! Having an "awareness of," while at the same time being "prepared for" will significantly help us on both sides of the equation. First being that we'll avoid the traps the enemy wants to catch us in. Secondly, that we'll clearly see the God-moments of our lives and be ready to step into them when they happen.

△△△

1. My TAKE AWAY from this chapter is...

2. This chapter makes me GRATEFUL because...

3. I will TAKE ACTION for this by...

2.12 | BEWARE OF DECEPTION

Beware of false prophets, who come to you in sheep's clothing but inwardly are ravenous wolves.

You will recognize them by their fruits...

So, every healthy tree bears good fruit, but the diseased tree bears bad fruit.
Matthew 7:15-17 ESV

Very hard yet undeniable truths in the passage above.

False prophets had long been a dangerous cancer in Israel's history. It is important to note that prophecy is delivered through two primary means of communication:

The first, *foretelling* (or predicting the future) tends to be the one we more readily consider.

The second means is just as important, *forth-telling* (or speaking on God's behalf.)

Both were used in their proper form by God's true prophets and leaders to guide and direct Israel into alignment with God's will. Alternatively, these so-called "false prophets" would manipulate these means of legitimate communication in order to satiate their own sordid desires and mislead God's people away from Him.

God's wrath is kindled against those who falsely pose as His voice piece. He can also get just as upset at those whose hearts and minds are gullible enough to fall for this deception. This is why we see God constantly warning Israel in the Old Testament and now His Church in the New.

Have you ever been sold a bill of goods by someone only to see the "wolf in sheep's clothing" exposed at some later time? This is where discernment and wisdom by testing is key. The Apostle John tells us how:

> **Beloved, do not believe every spirit, but test the spirits to see whether they are from God, for many false prophets have gone out into the world.**
>
> **1 John 4:1 ESV**

So, we are to "test" the quality of the words spoken. How do we do that? These two very simple tests have been proven particularly helpful to distinguish God's guidance from the misdirection of the enemy:

The first is to simply lay it alongside God's Word. Does it match up to what God has already said about Himself, sin, humanity, and this world? This, of course, requires that you "study {The Bible} to show yourself approved... accurately handling the word of truth." (See 2 Timothy 2:15.)

The second is to listen carefully as to what is being said about Jesus. Whenever Jesus' deity, humanity or authority is marginalized in any way—run away. Don't get caught up in this deception.

Whatever displaces your trust and faith in God, becomes your God.

There is still another vehicle of deception that we must beware: Ourselves. We all lie to ourselves at times, and we usually pay the price when all is said and done. How is it (and why is it) that we continue to trick ourselves? You would think the one person in the world you could be honest with is yourself!

Paul tells the church in Corinth something about this when he says:

> Let no one deceive himself. **If anyone among you seems to be wise in this age, let him become a fool that he may become wise.**
>
> **For the** wisdom of this world is foolishness **with God.**
>
> **1 Corinthians 3:18-19 NKJV**

To be humbly honest about what we don't know in order to seek guidance, counsel and help is all too rare a character trait these days. Don't pretend to know what you don't know. Learn to become more curious. This allows you time to process, as well "test the spirit."

Similarly, be true to yourself and to God. Can you picture the Holy Spirit sometimes just shaking His head in embarrassment for the lies that you tell yourself? Develop a habit of speaking God's truths instead. Warn yourself against the devious lies and threats that the enemy would have you believe.

> **Yes, and everyone who wants to live a godly life in Christ Jesus will suffer persecution.**
>
> **But** evil people and impostors will flourish. **They** will deceive others and will themselves be deceived.
>
> **But you must remain faithful to the things you have been taught. You know they are true, for you know you can trust those who taught you.**

One thing about Scripture. It sees the world as it really is. Evil. Nevertheless, we are empowered by God to be bright lights in this otherwise inescapable darkness. This takes wisdom, discernment and careful thought to our ways. If you want to truly, genuinely and authentically live for Jesus, it's going to cost you at one point or another. To be fair, this is true for anyone with any belief in anything.

We just have to decide the most viable and the most valuable object in which to place our faith.

There's nothing and no one else who has earned our allegiance more than Jesus Christ. It is up to every individual to decide how far they're going to take this eternally essential relationship. So beware of deception.

When misdirection, distraction and duplicity comes your way, how will you battle it? With what will you battle it? How you answer these questions for yourself will determine ultimately what and who you believe.

ΔΔΔ

1. My TAKE AWAY from this chapter is...

2. This chapter makes me GRATEFUL because...

3. I will TAKE ACTION for this by...

3.0 | JOY IN SERVING

JOY IN SERVING OTHERS

Therefore if you have any encouragement from being united with Christ, if any comfort from his love, if any common sharing in the Spirit, if any tenderness and compassion, then make my joy complete by being like-minded, having the same love, being one in spirit and of one mind.

Do nothing out of selfish ambition or vain conceit. Rather, in humility value others above yourselves, not looking to your own interests but each of you to the interests of the others.

Philippians 2:1-4 NIV

3.1 | TREAT OTHERS WELL

Treat others in the same way that you would want them to treat you.
Luke 6:31 NET

The above world-changing lifestyle philosophy is one of the most quoted principles of Jesus. It is set inside a more robust teaching that instructs us as to how we should treat our neighbors, our loved ones, and even our enemies. (We will cover all these in future chapters.) The line in the verse mentioned above however, is the fulcrum that places all the other parallel lessons—how we are to treat others—into balance.

The concept of "treating others as you would have them treat you" is all at once simple, profound, and yet still so very difficult to put into actual practice.

Why is that? Perhaps it is because we often look at the world through a "me-centered" lens. Meaning, we are usually so focused on what we expect from others, that we seldom consider how we go about our interactions with them.

Empathy has become a highly sought after character trait in our culture today, and rightly so. We each, as humans, have the innate desire to be heard and accurately understood. Think about a relationship you may currently have or have had in the past where the other person truly "got you."

Additionally, those who have learned how to empathize with others have also developed the ability to treat those same people in a gracious, patient and merciful manner.

Sadly, there are also those who know how to manipulate others by leveraging faux-empathy. Self-serving and shallow expressions of this kind usually end up hurting others in an even more disturbing way. The prophet Jeremiah speaks a direct word of God's anger at such people when He says:

> **They have** treated the brokenness of my dear people superficially, **claiming, "Peace, peace,"**
> **when there is no peace.**
> **Jeremiah 8:11 CSB**

Reaching out to others in a meagerly, superficial way can often add insult to injury. And, if we are to be candid, we have all been guilty of this at one point or another.

Why? Because it's hard to consistently model patience with someone else's brokenness.

This is why we must work to look at each other's hurts through the lens of our own past negative experiences. Doing this, we can plunge deep into the reservoir of our past tragedies to draw out hope, grace, comfort and mercy for those who find themselves in a similar state.

Before moving on, let's again add a measure of balance to this equation. Remember that we should discern and distinguish between those who are authentically kind versus those who would use kindness as a pretense.

David (before becoming King of Israel) had an opportunity to exact revenge against King Saul, but instead demonstrated an unexpected kindness. Even King Saul was humbled by this as he says:

> **"You are more righteous than I," he said.** "You have treated me well, **but** I have treated you badly.

The Lord delivered me into your hands, but you did not kill me.

When a man finds his enemy, does he let him get away unharmed? May the Lord reward you well for the way you treated me **today."**

1 Samuel 24:17-19 NIV

We learn from David that when you become known for treating everyone well, even those who treat you badly will be shamed into acknowledging your good character. When you have an opportunity for revenge, how will you respond? This will speak volumes to those around you, regardless of how they feel about you.

Both blessings and curses flow from how you engage and interact with others. Because of the law of reciprocity, how you treat people will serve as a faithful indicator of how they will come to treat you as well.

One last incentive in treating others well is that it teaches you to value others as they are, rather than merely what they can do for you. When we continually realize that all humans bear the image of Almighty God, it makes it that much easier to treat them in a way that honors God. Paul illustrates one type of this care:

For you know that we treated each of you as a father treats his own children—**encouraging you, comforting you, and urging you to walk in a manner worthy of God, who calls you into His own kingdom and glory.**

1 Thessalonians 2:11-12 BSB

Offering a heartfelt plea to the church at Thessalonica, Paul reminds them of how he and his ministry team treated them like a loving father and mentor. He speaks of encouragement and comfort, as well as challenging them to be the best versions of themselves. He then bridges those concepts to their own individual sense of worth and value.

"Value yourself. Value others. Allow others to value you. Bring value to others." Looking through the lens of value is a tremendous prompter for our actions, reactions and interactions with others.

How would you want to be treated in any given situation? Do you want grace and mercy? Show it to others. Do you want to be believed in? Believe in others. These examples and many like it are merely a few ways that we can treat others well.

△△△

1. My TAKE AWAY from this chapter is...

2. This chapter makes me GRATEFUL because...

3. I will TAKE ACTION for this by...

3.2 | JUDGE FAIRLY

Do not judge by appearance (superficially and arrogantly), but judge fairly and righteously.
John 7:24 AMP

We should all know this intuitively. As they say though, "common sense isn't common anymore."

Why then is this so very difficult? Having physical sight is one of our most useful tools as humans, but our eyes often betray sound thinking.

Our culture increasingly rushes to judgment in every arena. Many have lost the personal discipline of considering and processing the situations we encounter. Being taught *how* to think seems to have been dubiously displaced by being told *what* to think. When glancing superficially, we are sometimes arrogant enough to rush to snap judgments, even in the face of alternative explanations.

Jesus, in the narrative above, is right in the middle of being praised by some, questioned by others and still yet, hated by the rest. He points his listeners to several standards by which to guide their judgements. The first two we'll explore are tied to the concepts of "fairness" and "righteousness."

These two concepts, when juxtaposed, beg the question, "So, what is the standard for fairness and righteousness?" This is the very crux of Jesus' point. He is calling to those around Him to consider God's long-suffering as the lens for more thoughtful evaluation.

Next, we examine one more tool for making healthier judgments:

> Do not judge, **so that** you will not be judged.
>
> **For** in the way you judge, you will be judged; **and by your standard of measure, it will be measured to you.**
>
> **Matthew 7:1-2 NASB**

This particular passage has been one of the most mis-contextualized verses in all of Scripture. Due to the allowance on our part as believers, the world will often misuse this as a weapon against us.

"Don't judge me!" they say.

Then, quite often, dumb-founded silence on our part.

So, how should we respond? Think about it. Being told judgment is wrong is itself, a judgment. The very thing you're being told not to do! It is an inescapable logic that most do not even stop to consider.

Now that that's out of the way, let's see this verse for Jesus' intended use. It was meant as a prescription for exercising both "truth and grace." There is a striking contrast between judgment as a hateful expression of condemnation ("You're going to hell for that.") and judgment as a loving expression of warning ("You're better than that.")

That being said, there is an altogether shocking revelation that Paul shares with us regarding future events:

> **Do you not know that** the saints will judge the world**? And if the world is to be judged by you, are you Incompetent to try trivial cases?**

Do you not know that we are to judge angels**? How much more, then, matters pertaining to this life!**
1 Corinthians 6:2-3 ESV

How out-of-this-world are these claims by Paul!?

Just how will all of these events described above work out in the end? No idea. It seems intense though!

What we are to understand for now, is that if we are to judge the world and even the angels, how much more should we be able to judge everyday matters? Rather than taking altercations before a world system (which often rejects God and His truths), we should be able to settle disputes among ourselves in a way that honors God and seeks mutual benefit.

Lastly, when addressing the concept of judgment, it is vital that we understand it ultimately in the light of what is said about His Word. Jesus shares what seems to be an outrageously puzzling statement below when it comes to matters of truth, salvation, rejection and judgment:

I will not judge **those who hear Me but don't obey Me, for I have come to save the world and** not to judge it.

But all who reject Me and my message will be judged **on the day of judgment by the truth I have spoken.**
John 12:47-48 NLT

At first pass, this may come across as a contradictory statement. Jesus says in one verse that He's not going to judge, then in the next, it seems that He will. Again, while this may seem like a catch twenty-two, in reality it is one more example of His grace, mercy and patience with us.

How can this be? Because Christ was making it clear that His journey to the cross was the crowning pinnacle of His love for us. From this same cross comes our opportunity for forgiveness, salvation and entrance into Heaven.

However, the opportunity is always met with a choice. Our choice. Our choice to accept His offer. Our choice for what it means to escape the judgment of Hell to instead accept our Father's welcome into Heaven. But some may accuse, "How could a loving God send anyone to Hell?" The answer is simple. God doesn't want that at all. His offer of salvation stands as long as we have breath in in our bodies. (See Hebrews 9:27.)

God will never override the decisions of those who choose to reject Him. It's been said, "You have to push aside and almost trip over the bloody, broken body of His Son to end up in Hell."

As regarding judgment, we are to be patient, fair and righteous, as God is with His justice towards us. "Truth and grace" are the right and left arms of judgment. They were made to work in sync to pull others up, not push them down.

$$\triangle\triangle\triangle$$

1. My TAKE AWAY from this chapter is...

2. This chapter makes me GRATEFUL because...

3. I will TAKE ACTION for this by...

3.3 | LOVE ONE ANOTHER

This is My commandment, that you love one
another, **just as I have loved you.**

**Greater love has no one than this, that a person will
lay down his life for his friends.**
John 15:12-13 NASB

His disciples being utterly oblivious to all that was about to
unfold, Jesus foreshadows His own death with the statement
above. They were merely hours away from the final stage of
Christ's life-long journey to the cross. It is in this setting that we
hear Jesus' sincere appeal to the deepest possible expression of
love.

Referred to as *agape*, this sacrificial type of love is the strongest
of its kind because it prefers the well being of others over one's
self. Others, at the cost of you.

Serving as the ultimate fulfillment of this level of compassion
and commitment to others first, Christ challenges His disciples
to be ready to do the same. Jesus led by modeling perfectly the
example of how we are to love one another.

We are commanded to, time and time again, find love's ultimate
essence not only in what Jesus did, but also in the very sum and
substance of who God is:

Beloved, let us love one another, **for** love is of God;
and everyone who loves is born of God **and knows**
God.

He who does not love does not know God, **for God is love.**
1 John 4:7-8 NKJV

What a heavy statement! If we don't practice love, then we don't truly even know God (have a genuine relationship with Him.) So is God asking us to literally die for someone else to prove that we love them? To be sure, there are many that either have or at least have been willing to physically die for others. Selflessness to this degree deserves the highest of honors as well as unwavering admiration. This extreme display of love is rarely needed, yet we can show this same sacrificial (agape) love in a manifold number of other ways.

Much in the same way that we are called to "deny ourselves and take up our cross to follow Him," we are similarly commanded to lay down our own self-preservation and self-interests in order to lift others up.

Sometimes this expression of love is worked out in extreme ways. More often though, it is exemplified just as effectively in smaller, yet still meaningful doses. Paul shares a good example of this with the church at Rome:

Love one another **with brotherly affection. Outdo one another in showing honor.**
Romans 12:10 ESV

When was the last time you went out of your way to tangibly show honor to someone else? Paul challenges us to do this both personally as well as publicly.

Genuine affirmation of value is one of the most powerful ways of building trust in relationships.

Authentic demonstrations of honor become a trustworthy

indicator of how close-knit and heathy a community's culture really is.

Next, we will see another intriguing application of how we can show love for one another:

> **Let us think of ways to** motivate one another to acts of love **and good works.**
> **Hebrews 10:24 NLT**

When you truly love someone, you want them to prosper (see 3 John 1:1-6.) We can all testify that those around us who cared about our future, also pushed us in our present. Can you imagine how different this world would be if we "motivated" the good out of each other instead of provoking the bad?

What if we pulled one another closer toward the brink of love rather than pushing each other into the abyss of hate?

As we've learned, love's ultimate expression is personified in Christ. This same love then, is further proven as it flows from Him and into our own daily interactions with each other. Look at something else the Apostle John records of Jesus' words regarding love:

> **As I have loved you, so** you must love one another.
>
> **By this everyone will know that you are My disciples, if you** love one another.
> **John 13:34-35 NIV**

There you have it. The whole world is watching.

God is saying the world will know that we, as believers, are the real deal when and only when they see us love one another in the same way as Christ. The lifestyles of believers are always in view of both the courts of public opinion as well as the "great cloud of witnesses" in Heaven (see Hebrews 12:1). Jesus is making it abundantly clear that this particular command is how we're all being graded.

The call towards this type of sacrificial love is not merely a suggestion or a good idea in our Bibles. Loving one another is a holy expectation of God. We become worthy ambassadors for Christ when we faithfully operate through the empowerment and embodiment of the love of Christ.

△△△

1. My TAKE AWAY from this chapter is...

2. This chapter makes me GRATEFUL because...

3. I will TAKE ACTION for this by...

3.4 | LOVE YOUR NEIGHBOR

Now an expert in religious law stood up to test Jesus, saying, "Teacher, what must I do to inherit eternal life?"

He said to him, "What is written in the law? How do you understand it?"

The expert answered, "Love the Lord your God with all your heart, with all your soul, with all your strength, and with all your mind, and love your neighbor as yourself."

Jesus said to him, "You have answered correctly; do this, and you will live."

Luke 10:25-28 NET

Have you ever had an expert test you in the area of their given expertise? Few scenarios are more intimidating!

A religious lawyer and teacher was approaching Jesus with such a question. One we've all asked at one point, "What do I have do to get to Heaven?" Disappointingly, it seems that we humans secretly desire a different answer, though we're not quite sure what else it might be.

That being said, it is encouraging that the God of the Bible has never changed. Jesus simply responded in a way that was consistent with what this expert already knew—or at least should have. (See Deuteronomy 6:5 and Leviticus 19:18.)

Since we have dealt with the first part of this command in another session already (1.9 | Love God With All Your Being), we will focus in on the second part where Jesus instructs us to "love your neighbor as yourself."

What must be immediately caught in this re-assertion of the Old Testament by Christ is this:

How we treat others in our various circles of influence (aka our neighbors) is irrevocably tied to how we'll experience eternal life with Him. Furthermore, it also points to a preferable existence in the here and now.

Almost just as suddenly, our flesh or sin-nature seeks to qualify, justify and even attempt to negotiate who should be in the category of "neighbor", and who shouldn't be. This is nothing new. In fact, we see it here in the very next verse of the same narrative:

> **The man wanted to justify his actions, so he asked Jesus, "And who is my neighbor?"**
> **Luke 10:29 NLT**

Your neighbor won't always look like you, think like you, or live like you. So what do you do with that?

This is what the religious leader is beginning to learn from the parable that Jesus tells in the verses following. (See Luke 10:30-37.) Heaven is going to be filled with all types of people. If you don't know how to get along with those of a different color, background, tax bracket, or personality, you're going to hate it!

The love we are called to show our neighbors is emphasized with the qualifier of "as yourself."

> **If you fulfill the royal law as expressed in this scripture, "You shall love your neighbor as**

yourself," you are doing well.

But if you show prejudice, you are committing sin and are convicted by the law as violators.
James 2:8-9 NET

Why is this referred to as the "royal law?"

Because we achieve Kingdom-level majesty when we find the middle-ground between the mandate and the mindset to extend Christ-like patience, kindness, mercy and grace towards others. To live your life in this way is to rise above the noise and nastiness of this world.

There is simply no place at all for those representing Jesus Christ to be seen or heard expressing prejudice, hatred, gossip, slander, revenge, bitterness, or mean-spiritedness.

To be clear, we can still make our case in disagreements or disputes. It is in how we go about doing so that proves us to be fulfilling the command to love our neighbor, or not. Paul adds to this thought:

For you were called to freedom, brothers. Only do not use your freedom as an opportunity for the flesh, but through love serve one another.

For the whole law is fulfilled in one word: "You shall love your neighbor as yourself."
Galatians 5:13-14 ESV

After hearing difficult teachings like these, our responses are often comically predictable!

"But Jesus, you don't understand how they are or what they've done!" Or even, "Jesus, I hear you. I really do, but..."

Isn't it interesting how we often assume "worst-possible-case" scenario when others have seemed to say, done or even emote in a way that we didn't understand? Yet, when we misspeak, misunderstand or make a mistake, we crave mercy. We expect to be heard and understood in terms of the "best-possible-case?"

This is where the qualifying phrase "as yourself" holds so much revelatory power. Our love for our neighbor is to be a sacrificial love. Very much the same as what we owe to God. We are called to express this in a way that we would hope to be reciprocated, even when it isn't. Though it is not a gullible love, it is nonetheless a merciful, best-possible-case scenario expression.

We are commanded to leverage our freedom to serve others rather than allow them to suffer.

We do this in hopes that it will point them to the Jesus. The very one that has changed our lives and created a place of complete joy in us!

△△△

1. My TAKE AWAY from this chapter is...

2. This chapter makes me GRATEFUL because...

3. I will TAKE ACTION for this by...

3.5 | LOVE YOUR ENEMIES

But to those of you who will listen, I say: "Love your enemies, do good to those who hate you..."
Luke 6:27 BSB

As Christ-followers, we are always being called higher.

The mode and mood of lifestyle being described and commanded in this passage, by Jesus, is nothing short of ground-breaking. It devastates the preferences of the self. "Loving your enemies", serves as one of the most pivotal pieces of teachings that distinguishes us from the broken value systems of this world.

That being said, this command is incredibly difficult to practice consistently when real life opportunities—in the form of enemies—present themselves.

Yes, it sounds so perfectly spiritual, but have you ever really tried this when hatefulness comes knocking at your door? How about when someone else has made you, for whatever reason, their enemy? In the heat of the moment, it all just seems so nonsensical. Actually, it seems utterly ridiculous and even idiotic.

You see, we are creatures who have endured many kinds of pain. We don't like pain. Because of this, we've learned over time how to avoid it. How to guard ourselves from it. Even how to preemptively strike when we feel threatened. It's been said that, "Sometimes the best defense is a good offense."

Before you dismiss the notion, listen to something else that Jesus says. Something that is even more counter-intuitive:

> **But I say,** "Love your enemies! Pray for those who persecute you!
>
> **In that way, you will be acting as true children of your Father in Heaven. For He gives His sunlight to both the evil and the good, and He sends rain on the just and the unjust alike."**
> **Matthew 5:44-46 NLT**

Did you notice something above? We act most like a child of God when we act like our Heavenly Father. Redundant, I know. The logic however, is just so inescapable as it is also so much a gut-punch to our fleshly desire for revenge.

Jesus also makes an interesting case to love your enemy when He juxtaposes both the "evil" and the "good" people of this world. There seems to be an implication that we all have endured hate from others, in addition to being the one who has shown hate toward others. We all know what it feels like to have an enemy, as well as to be the enemy, whether justly labeled or not.

However easy it may be to take the lower road, remember, we are being called higher in our thinking compared to the rest of the world:

> **But** if you love those who love you, what credit is that to you**? For even sinners love those who love them.**
>
> **And if you do good to those who do good to you, what credit is that to you? For even sinners do the same.**
> **Luke 6:32-33 NKJV**

One can almost hear the patient tone in Christ's message with this teaching.

It's almost like He's saying, "Look, I get it. More than you know. I'm even about to show you that I practice what I preach. I'm about to go to the cross. Watch and learn from me. I'll show you how to demonstrate real love for your enemies, and even under the most extreme pressure."

There is a lot that goes into the level of trial and error that this teaching demands. Though, it is encouraging to learn that Jesus also builds in a reward to sweeten the deal. He knew we would need to feel a legitimate win, when we get this right. Listen to this encouragement to close out the thought:

> **But love your enemies and do good, and lend, expecting nothing in return; and your reward will be great, and you will be sons of the Most High; for He Himself is kind to ungrateful and evil people.**
> **Luke 6:35 NASB**

We started out in verse 27, where Jesus led off with, "But to those of you who will listen to me..."

Much like any other mentor when they specifically ask you to listen, they are about to raise the quality of your life. That is, *if* you heed their advice. But, that's not all. We're also taught that those who are willing to be called higher by "loving your enemy" can also expect to receive the reward that accompanies this type of commitment.

Perhaps this could even be one of the greatest gifts for a believer to receive. Why? Because once practiced well, God is solely responsible for the outcome that He's promised. Then, only He can be given the glory.

And why is this? Because it does not make sense—speaking after the manner of our sin nature—that we should benefit at all from actually practicing love for our enemies. This means that with worldly values such as, "Eat or be eaten" and "Survival of the fittest", it would seem rather like a recipe for our own destruction.

In the world's way of thinking, it doesn't compute to, "love your enemy" in the natural sense. That's because this is a supernatural principle.

However, in light of Heaven's economy and God's divine intervention, our efforts are powerfully blessed when we choose the higher road.

We will be learning how to genuinely forgive our enemies in a future session. For now, meditate on this command and let its teaching begin to take root in your heart.

Let's pray as the Psalmist prays to the Holy Spirit, "Search me… know me… test me…lead me…" (See Psalm 139:23-24.)

△△△

1. My TAKE AWAY from this chapter is…

2. This chapter makes me GRATEFUL because…

3. I will TAKE ACTION for this by…

3.6 | BE MERCIFUL

Be merciful, just as your Father is merciful.
Luke 6:36 NET

So, we have all experienced that moment of sheer embarrassment. Whether it was intentional or accidental. Whether it was through our hearing, our saying, our reacting, or even only in our thinking. Then, at some point, we suddenly realized how wrongly we "read the room."

How kind would it have felt to be shown some genuine mercy in that very moment? What's said of mercy often rings true: "We all want mercy when we goof up, but we are not near as ready to offer it to others when they do the same."

In this section of the book so far, we've learned about how we should treat others. We've also discovered what it means to judge rightly. And for the last few sessions, we've developed an appreciation for loving others at three important levels:

Those who believe the same as us.

Those who believe differently.

And those who can't stand us (or maybe even, vice versa.)

If there is any fulcrum, any balance, any hinge on which the pendulum swings between judgment and love, it is in the concept of what we refer to as *mercy*.

Fantastically enough, we are indeed empowered to be merciful in a way that mirrors our Heavenly Father. He freely offers mercy to all who would ask Him. Similarly, we are called to offer it towards others, in the same way and with the same gusto. What does this mean?

One can easily sense the loving anticipation in the passage below. God seems to be counting down the days to the point where the death, burial and resurrection of His Son would restore a relationship that had been broken for millennia:

> **"Behold, days are coming," says the Lord, "when I will bring about a new covenant."**
>
> **"For** I will be merciful **toward their wrongdoings, and** their sins I will no longer remember.**"**
> **Hebrews 8:8, 12 NASB**

How does one precisely define mercy? And is it the same thing as grace? The above passage helps considerably. It's been said that, "Mercy is not getting what you do deserve (God's wrath) while grace is getting something you do not deserve (God's blessing)."

As a believer we experience this as God has chosen to cover our wrongdoings. Jesus even invokes this sentiment to the extent of Himself having "divine amnesia" in regard to our sins!

There are, however, two pre-qualifications before we can experience this type of limitless mercy.

First and most obvious, we must be authentically repentant.

Second, we must commit to the practice of becoming dedicated dispensaries of mercy ourselves.

The Apostle James makes the case:

> **For judgment is without mercy to the one who has not shown mercy.** Mercy triumphs over judgment.
> **James 2:13 CSB**

This is a stark reminder in how seriously God takes the issue of mercy. We see here that it is elevated over judgment itself! Have you ever been able to let a spirit of mercy win out over a spirit of judgment in your life? How refreshing and empowering was that?

Diving a little deeper into the illustration James presents, the use of the word "triumph" points to spiritual warfare itself. This carries with it truly astounding implications.

Showing mercy, when it would be so much easier to pass judgement, is one of the most Christ-like things we can do!

Both parties experience a victory that would otherwise be undeserved and unrealized. Being merciful is a display of spiritual strength, rather than weakness. Listen to the words of the prophet Micah:

> **He hath shewed thee, O man, what is good; and what doth the LORD require of thee, but to do justly, and to love mercy, and to walk humbly with thy God?**
> **Micah 6:8 KJV**

Christ has truly shown us what is good. He doesn't make it complicated, as we sometimes wrongly ascribe to Him. Above, Micah is speaking under the leading of the Holy Spirit when he simply says, "Do the right thing, show mercy to others and be humble about it."

How interesting it is that "walk humbly" was added after the other two points. Maybe it was just a general statement about being humble? Or maybe it was meant to be tied to the idea of showing mercy, while also not gloating in the process? Decide what you think about that, but it works out either way you slice it.

Scripture is brilliant that way.

In conclusion, consider the abundant mercy God has shown you over the course of your life. Now, in light of that, consider how you can show this same mercy to others. When mercy wins, we all win.

Picture for a moment what media, social media, family gatherings, churches, businesses and the whole world for that matter would look like if there was simply a little more... mercy.

△△△

1. My TAKE AWAY from this chapter is...

2. This chapter makes me GRATEFUL because...

3. I will TAKE ACTION for this by...

3.7 | TURN THE OTHER CHEEK

Bless those who curse you, pray for those who mistreat you.

If someone slaps you on one cheek, turn to them the other also...

Luke 6:28-29 NIV

We are sure you've noticed by now how rich Luke 6 and Matthew 5 are when it comes to Jesus' teachings on how to act, react, and interact in a way that honors Him. What is just as interesting to note is how powerful they are in the realm of spiritual warfare.

It's been said that, "You can't ever prove somebody wrong by proving them right."

We know that almost everyone naturally feels compelled to respond to persecution with rage and revenge. Again, this is natural, which is why Christ's command here stands apart as supernatural. It rises high above what most would normally do when their Christian faith or lifestyle is met with resistance.

Another important factor to this type of command is found in the *when.* When exactly is "turning the other cheek" the most appropriate response? While it could be leveraged effectively in many situations in a way that would bring glory to God, we must also be wise.

As principles within Ecclesiastes teach us, there are times when defending ourselves is the right course of action. Sometimes we take a stand and sometimes we are called to suffer persecution.

We must be prayerful and discerning of our *when.*

Understand that practicing our faith is very much in the same vein as a doctor who practices medicine. Will we always get it right? No. This is why we look to the Holy Spirit's guidance, Scripture, godly counsel, as well as drawing on whatever experiences we've had throughout our faith journey.

We see Matthew expand on this command by comparing it to an Old Testament mandate on Israel's culture:

> **You have heard that it was said, "An eye for an eye and a tooth for a tooth."**
>
> **But I tell you not to resist an evil person. But** whoever slaps you on your right cheek, turn the other to him also.
> **Matthew 5:38-39 NKJV**

So we are soundly commanded against taking revenge of our own accord. However again, it is key to grasp why Christ is calling us to do something so difficult.

First, "turning the other cheek," along with similar illustrations in verses 40-41 (which we'll discuss in future chapters), serves as a disciplining of oneself to not regard anything in this world as high as the hope we hold in Christ. We place our pride, our pettiness and our possessions all on the chopping block when compared to our faith in Christ.

Second, partnering in Christ's sufferings by taking punishment for the sake of His Name is one of the highest honors of the believer. We are to "leave room for God's wrath" (Romans 12:19) and not give room for our own. This takes extreme discipline. Try it the next time you're insulted for simply sharing your love for Jesus. It truly makes you feel closer to God when you're insulted for His sake.

The prophet Jeremiah understood this centuries before, when he teaches us through the leading of the Holy Spirit:

> Let them turn the other cheek **to those who strike them and** accept the insults of their enemies.
>
> **For no one is abandoned by the Lord forever.**
>
> **Though He brings grief, He also shows compassion because of the greatness of His unfailing love.**
> **Lamentations 3:30-32 NLT**

How provocative it is that this prophet is making a connection between the grief that Israel suffered (as a temporary form of God's judgment) for their own sins as a nation! Could this be why we sometimes experience seasons of persecution or suffering? Maybe or maybe not, but it's worth an honest moment of reflection.

Jeremiah also seems to be working from the premise that if our present circumstances has produced grief by someone else's hand, that this could be an occasion that ultimately draws us closer to God's compassion and deliverance.

In the following passage, Isaiah actually predicts the suffering of Jesus. Notice His response to the abuse, shame and grief that was still centuries away from being fulfilled:

> I gave My back to those who strike, **and My cheeks to those who pull out the beard;** I hid not My face **from disgrace and spitting.**
>
> **But the Lord GOD helps Me; therefore I have not been disgraced; therefore** I have set My face like a flint, **and I know that I shall not be put to shame.**
>
> **He who vindicates Me is near.**

Look at how our Messiah was to suffer! Yet He still came to save us. Something so beautiful and so encouraging is to understand that Jesus will never ask us to endure something that He hasn't already Himself.

He can identify with persecution because He Himself was persecuted. We see Him epitomize and model perfectly how to "turn the other cheek."

△△△

1. My TAKE AWAY from this chapter is...

2. This chapter makes me GRATEFUL because...

3. I will TAKE ACTION for this by...

3.8 | MIND YOUR ANGER

I say to you that everyone who is angry with his
brother will be liable to judgment; **whoever
insults his brother... and whoever says, "You
fool!" will be liable to the hell of fire.**

Matthew 5:22 ESV

We enter into a particular grouping of commands in Scripture
where we hear Jesus repeating a formula that both qualifies and
calls us to a deeper level of living. He says, "You have heard
it said... but I say to you..." With this simple construct, we
undoubtedly feel the bar being raised as He speaks.

Jesus is warning us that anger can become a devastating liability
in the life and witness of the believer. He drills down to the core
of our sinful tendencies in commanding us to guard how we
treat and speak to others when we are angry.

And, curiously enough, we have an incredibly consistent God.
Look at what He says all the way back in the book of Genesis, to
the second generation of humankind:

> "Why are you so angry?" **the LORD asked Cain.**
> "Why do you look so dejected?
>
> **You will be accepted if you do what is right. But if
> you refuse to do what is right, then watch out!** Sin
> is crouching **at the door, eager to control you. But**
> you must subdue it and be its master."

Genesis 4:6-7 NLT

First notice the reflective question that God poses to Cain. Could you imagine how different and how much control we could exercise over our own lives, if we would just pause a beat to ask ourselves, "Why am I so angry?"

Second, when we develop the discipline of identifying the real root of our anger, we gain the precious time needed to get ourselves under control. What an incredible insight God offers us into the psychology between anger and our acting upon it when He says, "Sin is crouching at your door... and you must master it."

Look at the proverbial results of a failure to do so:

> **An** angry man stirs up strife, **And a** hot-tempered
> **and undisciplined man commits many**
> **transgressions.**
> **Proverbs 29:22 AMP**

So we see that anger—unchecked and undisciplined—will cause us to cross lines that can ruin our witness for God as well as our relationships with others. Like a wrecking ball to the corner support of a building, a hot temper can cause irreversible damage and destruction.

This being said, the goal is not to repress anger by our own power, but instead to bring our anger under the submission of the Holy Spirit. Additionally, Paul directs us:

> Be angry and do not sin; **do not let the sun go down**
> **on your anger, and** give no opportunity to the
> devil.
> **Ephesians 4:26-27 ESV**

This verse is profound in many ways and yet has been often

misunderstood in perhaps one of its applications.

As far as what should already be clear, our anger should never be used as an excuse for sin. The enemy is always looking for the opportunity to divide friends, families, churches and the like. We must, as far as we are able, never allow our angst to be the reason for division.

Now, as far as what is sometimes misunderstood, look at the phrase, "do not let the sun go down on your anger." The often-pointed-to application of this is usually in the context of marriages and not going to bed mad at each other.

While this is a helpful notion when possible, it is not always practical. Some people need longer to "cool off." That's their business. What would be most helpful is to re-read the line with emphasis, "do not let the sun go down on *your* anger." Your anger is the only one that you can control. This should point you to prayer, repentance and to commit to forgiving the other party in your heart.

James further gives us a brilliantly inspired teaching on how to have the "crucial conversation" that is often needed when dealing with anger:

> **Understand this, my dear brothers and sisters: You must all be quick to listen, slow to speak, and** slow to get angry.
>
> Human anger does not produce the righteousness **God desires.**
> **James 1:19-20 NLT**

How different would your life be—right now—if your initial reaction was to listen first, then speak? (We mean actually listen first, not just wait for your turn to speak.) Pushing the principle further, how often would you have even gotten angry if you had simply stayed curious a little longer and given the other person time to talk through the matter?

Unbridled and unyielded anger has been one of the most devastating epidemics of humankind. This has been true even since our very beginnings. Anger has been responsible for the most unspeakable of tragedies and horrific levels of destruction.

Remember that God calls us towards peace and to be peace-makers whenever and wherever possible.

△△△

1. My TAKE AWAY from this chapter is...

2. This chapter makes me GRATEFUL because...

3. I will TAKE ACTION for this by...

3.9 | FORGIVE OTHERS

If you forgive those who sin against you, **your Heavenly Father will forgive you.**

But if you refuse to forgive others, **your Father will not forgive your sins.**
Matthew 6:14-15 NLT

This has got to be one of the most in-your-face commands with which Christ confronts our hearts. Everything in our being furiously fights against forgiving others.

Did you catch the severe warning about holding unforgiveness in your heart? It's quite clear that if we don't forgive others, He won't forgive us. We are left with no wiggle room.

Sometimes we avoid this truth. Why? Because many of us have been hurt badly by others. Taken even further, some of us have been damaged by others more than once. Can you imagine Peter's facial expression as Christ responds to his question?

Then Peter came up and said to Him, "Lord, how often will my brother sin against me, and I forgive him? **As many as seven times?"**

Jesus said to him, "I do not say to you seven times, but seventy-seven times."
Matthew 18:21-22 ESV

Context is everything, so let's pair this with Jesus' warnings "not to cast our pearls before swine" (Matt 7:6) as well as the equally pointed proverb, "a dog returns to his vomit..." (See Proverbs 26:11 / 2 Peter 2:22.)

We add this balance because there can sometimes be a misunderstanding of Jesus' intent. Being willing to forgive someone is not the same as becoming their "doormat."

Forgiveness has nothing to do with weakness. In fact, it is best understood through the lens of strength. How is that? Because to forgive someone, you have to clearly confront the wrong that was done. This takes guts.

Simultaneously, biblical forgiveness is first about releasing someone from the weight of their sin. This is true whether it was against you, someone else you care about or even God. Secondly, it is calling out that what was done was, in fact, wrong. Then setting clear boundaries as all parties involved move forward.

Jesus was challenging Peter's thinking, and by extension our own, into reminding us of how much we've wronged God. Yet, He still loves and forgives us.

When we refuse to balance mercy and patience alongside discernment and discretion, we rob ourselves of God's blessing. We may even be guilty of forcing His wrath on us, as we see in the ending lines of this parable of Jesus:

And because he was angry, his master handed him over to the jailers to be tortured until he could pay everything that was owed.

So also my Heavenly Father will do to you unless every one of you forgives his brother or sister from your heart.
Matthew 18:34-35 CSB

The main take away here is the qualifying clause, "from your heart." The offending party may want to continue to offend. Let them. (You can't always control that anyways.)

Your role as a Christ-follower is to become unoffendable. When you—empowered by the Holy Spirit—can rise to this challenge, people who mean you harm, will no longer exercise power over you. Paul expands on this idea of being unoffendable:

> **Therefore, as the elect of God, holy and dearly loved, clothe yourselves with a heart of mercy, kindness, humility, gentleness, and patience, bearing with one another and forgiving one another, if someone happens to have a complaint against anyone else. Just as the Lord has forgiven you, so you also forgive others.**
>
> **Colossians 3:12-13 NET**

Now, as a break from the normal flow of this book, let's attempt something daring:

Think of someone, at some point in your life who has hurt you in some deep way. Hold that thought. (Don't hurry this process.)

And now, pause and think of the worst thing that you have ever done. It's a heavy thought, we understand. When you did this, you made yourself an enemy against Christ and His Kingdom. There's no candy-coating it.

Next, picture Christ's tear-stained smile as He dies on the cross. Just for you. Just so He could erase your offense against Him. Do you deserve to be forgiven? No, but He made the choice to free you anyways. How does it feel to not be held hostage by your mistakes any longer? Can you begin to feel His rich, lavish, kind and undeserved love?

(Good, remember this same love because you're about to give it to someone else who doesn't deserve it.)

Last, with just you and God in the space of your head and heart, think back to the person you originally had in mind. The one who wronged you.

Before your blood begins to boil with anger or hurt, think back again to that picture of Jesus locking eyes with you from the cross. Now, see your enemy through Christ's eyes for a moment, and picture yourself, through Christ, forgiving them. Fight through the anger, rage, confusion, disappointments—all of it. Tell them simply and from your heart:

"I forgive you."

Were you unable to follow through? Was it too difficult for you? Try it again and ask the Holy Spirit to help you. This is too important and the stakes are too high.

Don't let God's forgiveness of your sins be blocked by your lack of forgiveness for others.

Or, were you able to genuinely forgive? If you did, congratulations! Not only have you set them free but even more satisfying is the fact that you have been set free. How's that you ask? Because that offense no longer has any power over you.

Whenever struggling with unforgiveness, remember: "The forgiven, forgive."

ΔΔΔ

1. My TAKE AWAY from this chapter is...

2. This chapter makes me GRATEFUL because...

3. I will TAKE ACTION for this by...

3.10 | GO AND BE RECONCILED

Therefore if you bring your gift to the altar, and there remember that your brother has something against you, leave your gift there before the altar, and go your way. First be reconciled to your brother, and then come and offer your gift.
Matthew 5:23-24 NKJV

Pop quiz: How many times have you read the above passage and mistakenly switched the roles of who was the *offender* and the *offended*?

Similar to what's known as the "Mandela effect," many believers are shocked to realize that this passage is not about us forgiving someone else for a wrong they've done to us. It's quite the reverse, whether in reality or in perception.

Why is this important? Where or when does this apply? This is important because—as far as we are able—we must strive towards peace with everyone. In a society and culture that continues to more stubbornly entrench itself in the mantra of "I'm right and you're wrong," Jesus is calling us to a better way.

We are charged to make a genuine effort of attempting to "make things right" over and above the prideful notion of "being right." This is what is meant by "go and be reconciled."

For the sake of balance, it is also helpful to understand this command is expressly for those who are like-minded in their faith in Christ. Why? Because they are called, as a fellow believer, to respond with forgiveness. This way God can be given the glory on both accounts. Additionally, both parties can become blameless again as they approach God in prayer and in worship.

But what about those who are not Christ-followers? There is an answer and solid reasoning for reconciliation here as well:

Why don't you judge for yourselves what is right?

As you are going with your adversary to the magistrate, try hard to be reconciled on the way, or your adversary may drag you off to the judge, and the judge turn you over to the officer, and the officer throw you into prison.

Luke 12:57-58 NIV

So, now we are examining what it looks like to be reconciled with those who would make themselves our enemies (or to be fair, maybe someone of whom we've made an enemy.) The logic behind making things right is crystal clear:

You would be wise to work toward reconciliation so it doesn't destroy your bank account, your life, your reputation, your influence or your locale.

It is true that we can't control our enemies possible desires to destroy us in some cases. Counterintuitively, it might also be beneficial to acknowledge that a desire to more quickly "go and be reconciled" on our part, could possibly save years of litigation, many tears and otherwise bitter disputes.

The following proverb doubles down on the effect of humility and peace-seeking:

When a person's ways are pleasing to the LORD, he even reconciles his enemies to himself.

Proverbs 16:7 NET

In this proverb, there is the slightest hint that this type of lifestyle enjoys reconciliation from a place of strength. (As opposed to the Luke 12 passage which seems to be from a place of weakness.)

Either way, we undoubtedly see the secret ingredient of the Holy Spirit bringing empowerment and favor to the lives of those who will heed this command of Christ. Paul unpacks this concept even more to reveal how special it is to be entrusted with the message and ministry of reconciliation.

> **All this is from God, who through** Christ reconciled us to Himself **and** gave us the ministry of reconciliation; **that is, in** Christ God was reconciling the world **to Himself, not counting their trespasses against them, and** entrusting to us the message of reconciliation.
>
> **Therefore, we are ambassadors for Christ...**
> **2 Corinthians 5:18-20 ESV**

True reconciliation finds its ultimate origin, definition, expression and application in Almighty God Himself.

He gave us the supreme example of this through Christ's reconciling our relationship to God through the cross. Said very simply, Jesus made things right again between us and God.

Knowing this, we should be both humbled and moved to do the same, as best as we are able. As we've discovered, this teaching holds true for both our brothers/sisters in Christ, in addition to our enemies.

Again, we can't dictate to others how they should feel, react or even what to believe about us. We can, however, remove their excuses when we exercise a Christ-like love and resolve to "go and be reconciled."

Paul contends with his readers that we are, in fact, ambassadors for Christ in this world, representing Him everywhere we go. This demands that we hold in high esteem the message and ministry of reconciliation. It is something we've been entrusted and expected to do.

What a responsibility! What a privilege!

∆∆∆

1. My TAKE AWAY from this chapter is...

2. This chapter makes me GRATEFUL because...

3. I will TAKE ACTION for this by...

3.11 | GUARD AGAINST LUST

You have heard the commandment that says, "You must not commit adultery."

But I say, "anyone who even looks at a woman with lust has already committed adultery **with her in his heart."**
Matthew 5:27-28 NLT

Our hearts: That's what matters most to God.

The Old Testament command against adultery served only as a deterrent to the act. However, Jesus goes deeper to address the heart decisions often made way before the act is even committed. It is truly terrifying to realize that God holds us accountable for giving into our sinful lusts, even when only in our hearts.

Scripture is clear. Lust is sin.

While the example above is speaking of a man lusting after a woman that is not his wife, there is a whole spectrum of ways lust can latch on to us. Our money, possessions, fame and relationships will all be tempted by lust. God even equated lust with idolatry when passing judgment on Israel.

The apostle James (also Jesus' half-brother) provides some illuminating insight into how lust works inside of us, if not dealt with quickly:

> **But each one is tempted when he is** carried away
> and enticed by his own lust.
>
> **Then** when lust has conceived, it gives birth to sin;
> **and sin, when it has run its course, brings forth
> death.**
> **James 1:14-15 NASB**

So, as James teaches, there should be a clear distinction made between "temptation" and "lust."

Temptation isn't sin in and of itself, but rather the prerequisite *urge* to sin. Think of it like an itch that you can't stop thinking about scratching.

The word picture James gives us regarding lust is that it is "conceived and giving birth." This is a perfect metaphor for when our human will allows the destructive spiritual seed of lust to take root. This is why lust is never satisfied and will continue to grow inside of us until it destroys us.

You may be saying, "Well, that all sounds terrible! So how am I supposed to overcome lust?" Paul gives Timothy the best kind of advice when he says:

> **Run away from youthful lusts--pursue
> righteousness, faith, love, and peace with those
> [believers] who call on the Lord out of a pure
> heart.**
> **2 Timothy 2:22 AMP**

Yes. That's right. When it comes to lust... run away!

Nearly everywhere else in Scripture we are told to take a stand. Not when it comes to lust however. Remove yourself from the situation as quickly as you possibly can (and vice versa if more applicable.) Also just as practical as what we need to run from, Paul tells us what we should run towards.

Passionately pursue the right things and then you won't be tempted to chase after the wrong things. Get accountability partners in our lives! Pursue friends who will lift you up rather than pull you down.

And, if you're wondering if your "old friends" will understand this "new you" in Christ, Peter tells us while there is a chance, we shouldn't hold our breaths in hope:

> You have had enough **in the past of the evil things that godless people enjoy—their** immorality and lust**, their feasting and drunkenness and wild parties...**
>
> **Of course, your former friends are surprised when you no longer plunge into the flood of wild and destructive things they do. So they slander you.**
> **1 Peter 4:3-4 NLT**

Don't expect someone to understand your new freedom in Christ while they're still imprisoned by their own lusts.

But "you have had enough" of it, as Peter so pointedly states, and that old life is not for you anymore. You're being called higher. You are pursuing a joy that is on command.

Sure, they may make fun of you. Let them. More than likely, it's due to the old cliché that "misery loves company." You won't be there with them doing those things anymore. They know how miserable and dissatisfied lusts leaves them and now they will have one less partner to share the heavy burden of sin's consequences.

Show them mercy paired with wisdom because:

We too were once... enslaved to various lusts and pleasures...

But when the kindness of God our Savior... appeared, He saved us... in accordance with His mercy, by the washing of regeneration and renewing by the Holy Spirit...
Titus 3:3-5 NASB

Take hope that your boldness will be a bright light shining to inspire others to break free from bonds of lust. Pray for them while showing gratitude to the Holy Spirit for helping you conquer sin in your own life.

What a kindness indeed that God saved us!

Not only from the ultimate hell to come, but from the hell that lust can create in our day-to-day lives. As Christ followers, we have been regenerated and renewed to experience power over the enslavement of the enemy as we guard against lust.

△△△

1. My TAKE AWAY from this chapter is...

2. This chapter makes me GRATEFUL because...

3. I will TAKE ACTION for this by...

3.12 | TAKE HEED

Then He said to them, "Take heed what you hear. **With the same measure you use, it will be measured to you; and to you who hear, more will be given.**

For whoever has, to him more will be given; but whoever does not have, even what he has will be taken away from him."
Mark 4:24-25 NKJV

Take heed.

These two little words embody a challenge from Scripture that employs disciplined engagement, alignment and coordination. The from our spirit, soul, mind and body altogether. Faithfulness to this command of Jesus is the result of what it means to have mastery over the self and total surrender to the Holy Spirit.

To "take heed" is to acknowledge and apply the sum total of all Jesus' teachings.

This is also one of those commands that comes with a powerful if/then promise. What Jesus is proposing should be incredibly motivating to all believers. He's saying, "Use what you've already been given, and I'll give you more. But if you don't, I won't (and you'll even lose what you've got!)" So, whether it's positive or negative reinforcement that moves you, Jesus has something to say about it.

As already mentioned, to "take heed" can translate into a spectrum of applications in our lives. Let's explore this next way, which cautions us in our thought life and the temptations that come our way:

> **Therefore let anyone who thinks that he stands take heed lest he fall.**
>
> **No temptation has overtaken you that is not common to man. God is faithful, and He will not let you be tempted beyond your ability, but with the temptation He will also provide the way of escape, that you may be able to endure it.**
> **1 Corinthians 10:12-13 ESV**

In the above example, we quickly see the connection to raise awareness in order to guard ourselves against the sin of pride, lust and weakness. What is encouraging to hear is that this is "common to man." Meaning that though difficult, it's also been overcome by others before.

Find someone who's been through what you're going through and seek their help in getting your breakthrough!

However difficult the temptation may be, God also promises that He will always provide a means of escape. God does not want you getting tripped up in your faith journey. That being said, it also takes endurance and self-discipline on your part. This holds true before, during and after moments of challenge arise in your life.

Next, we shift to the discipline of constant awareness and anticipation of the Lord's return:

> **But of that day and hour no one knows, not even the angels in heaven, nor the Son, but only the Father.**

> Take heed, watch and pray; **for you do not know when the time is.**
> **Mark 13:32-33 NKJV**

We're not the first generation of the church that thought God would come back during their time on earth, but it is always possible that we may indeed be the last. That's the very tension God imposed upon humanity so that we would not become complacent in our faith.

In fact, this is one of the reasons that Paul had to correct the thinking, theology and laziness within the church of Thessalonica. (See 2 Thessalonians.) They were acting like nothing on earth mattered anymore because Christ was coming back within months or even weeks. Rather than it stirring up a sense of urgency, they used it as an excuse to quite literally do nothing.

In similar fashion, Paul sternly warns the church at Colosse to be mindful to keep the work of ministry moving forward:

> Take heed to the ministry that you have received **in the Lord, that you may fulfill it.**
> **Colossians 4:17 BLB**

As followers of Christ, we have the privilege of taking the gifting, calling and relationships we've received from the Lord and discovering how we can best fulfill God's purpose through them.

God's gift of salvation is the gift that keeps on giving, bearing more fruit in each consecutive season of the church. Past generations, as well as future ones are counting on our active participation of the command to "take heed," more so than just our mere acceptance of it.

As we close this section of the book, you have been given

powerful tools to get your relationship with God in order (sections one and two.) You have now been equipped to sort out your heart and your differences with others (section three.)

Why does all this matter? Because as you've said yes to this journey, you have truly become Christ's disciple and are beginning to show real, spiritual fruit in your life.

You have already been learning how to authentically and meaningfully model your faith in Christ. Now, as we move into section four, you will be emboldened and equipped to effectively and accurately share your faith with others.

ΔΔΔ

1. My TAKE AWAY from this chapter is...

2. This chapter makes me GRATEFUL because...

3. I will TAKE ACTION for this by...

JOY IN SHARING GOD WITH OTHERS

But you shall be called the priests of the LORD; they shall speak of you as the ministers of our God...

Instead of your shame there shall be a double portion; instead of dishonor they shall rejoice in their lot; therefore in their land they shall possess a double portion; they shall have everlasting joy.

Isaiah 61:6-7 ESV

4.1 | SET THE EXAMPLE

I have set you an example that you should do as I have done for you.

Very truly I tell you, no servant is greater than his master, nor is a messenger greater than the one who sent him.

Now that you know these things, you will be blessed if you do them.
John 13:15-17 NIV

As we look to Jesus, there is no one in the history of human existence that has more right to give the "Do as I tell you" speech. Even more remarkable, the testimony of His life itself also preaches to us, "Do as you've seen me do."

(Quite the comical contrast from the rest of us whose lives often read more like, "Do as I say and not as I do.")

And it's in this artery of Christianity itself that the life's blood of our faith is fueled. Whatever we might suffer or experience, Christ can sympathize with us. He's right there with us in the middle of every trial and temptation. Through following His example, we can turn any negative situation into a triumph for His glory and for the building up of our faith.

While it is certainly true that we have Christ as the ultimate example, ask yourself additionally if you have anyone else in your life who models well what it means to be a Christ follower? Someone you can look to for guidance.

Paul was confident to say this to his churches:

> ...follow my example, **as I** follow the example of
> Christ.
>
> **1 Corinthians 11:1 CEV**

Now, there is a Grand Canyon's worth of difference between trying to portray a fake, self-righteous image of the "perfect" Christian, as opposed to being confident enough that the example you're setting inspires others to a higher level of faith. Due to the former, there has been a tragic loss of trust among some high-level pastors, priests and other clergy world-wide.

Fallen moments like these cause quite a bit of damage to Christ's body. This is why we should never place our faith fully in man.

This is also why Paul was humble enough to add the qualifier of "as I follow Christ." He made it clear to his reader that he himself is under subjection to Christ and also subject to his own shortcomings. Our spiritual leaders are human just like us. They will fail. May they be granted the same level of grace and mercy as they seek restoration for any wrong! (And the same mercy that they often have given us when we fail.)

Sometimes, setting the example comes at the cost of taking a stand in the midst of opposition. James tells us:

> Brothers and sisters, as an example **of patience in
> the face of suffering...**
>
> **We count as blessed those who have persevered.
> You have heard of Job's perseverance and have
> seen what the Lord finally brought about.**
>
> **James 5:10-11 NIV**

Have you ever considered how much we tend to revere people

who have gone through a lot in life, but somehow still keep it together? We imagine ourselves, even if for a fleeting moment, in their shoes and wonder how in the world we would make it through something like that!

God sees all that you're going through. Stay faithful and make up your mind to set a good example, even in the worst of times. He's promised He'll bless you for your perseverance!

Paul builds on what we've learned from James:

> **In everything,** show yourself to be an example by doing good works. **In your teaching show integrity, dignity, and wholesome speech that is above reproach, so that anyone who opposes us will be ashamed, having nothing bad to say about us.**
>
> **Titus 2:7-8 BSB**

"Being an example" means that you're actually *doing* something about it. Intentions aren't enough. Your Christ-like example must be heard, felt, seen and proven consistent over time. Our goal is not for anyone to feel shame, however when we get this right, people will have to think twice before talking about us behind our backs.

Why? Because when a toxic person tries to spew venom about someone else known to be a genuinely good person, most everyone can see right through it!

There is something to be said about a life well-lived:

> ...you became examples to all... **who believe.**
>
> **For from you the word of the Lord has sounded forth... in every place. Your faith toward God has gone out, so that we do not need to say anything.**

The godly impact of your life has the potential to go out ahead of you into every area of your life. There is a truth to the saying, "Your reputation proceeds you." Your example could quite literally affect people you will never meet this side of Heaven.

Be mindful to set the right example. One that reflects the wisdom, love, joy and glory of God. How you live today determines who you'll be tomorrow.

Choose wisely. Attract people to the Jesus that you call your Savior. Let them not only hear about Jesus from you, but let them experience Him through you. As the old saying goes, "More is caught, than taught."

△△△

1. My TAKE AWAY from this chapter is...

2. This chapter makes me GRATEFUL because...

3. I will TAKE ACTION for this by...

4.2 | SHINE YOUR LIGHT

You are the light of the world. A city set on a hill cannot be hidden.

Nor do people light a lamp and put it under a basket, but on a stand, and it gives light to all in the house.

In the same way, let your light shine before others, so that they may see your good works and give glory to your Father who is in Heaven.

Matthew 5:14-16 ESV

What an incredible purpose! What a beautiful calling!

We were born again to be "light" and then we are called to "let our light shine." A flashlight in the dark is only useful when it has a power source, when it is flipped to the on position and when the light it casts is unimpeded. So it is with our witness of Jesus Christ. There are several powerful word-pictures being presented in this command.

First, the community of God—Christ's followers—should live their lives at an elevated level. Mind you, we are not meaning this in a way that comes across as "holier than thou," but rather as a beacon for others in search of hope.

Second, your Christlike love and life-example should be on display for all that are in your house. When our walk with God only exists in the one to two hour setting of a Sunday morning, the most important relationships in our lives won't buy it. Those in our homes and families should be the primary recipients of the light and love that we cast.

Third, there is an inseparable link Jesus makes between "shining our light" and our "good works." When we're passionate about the former (shining our light), the latter (our good works) more readily flow out of us with the pure motive of bringing glory to God and not to ourselves.

Earlier we mentioned the power source for the light we are to shine. The Apostle John points us to Jesus:

> **The Word gave life to everything that was created, and His life brought light to everyone.**
>
> **The light shines in the darkness, and the darkness can never extinguish it.**
> **John 1:4-5 NLT**

Jesus is the power source of the true light through which we become capable of shining in this world. Being the ultimate Word, Light, and Life, Jesus empowers us to outshine the darkest of situations that we might ever encounter. The light of Christ can never be overcome, extinguished or conquered.

Of course, this is only an accurate statement in our lives so long as we actually reflect His glory rather than sin:

> **So that no one can criticize you. Live clean, innocent lives as children of God, shining like bright lights in a world full of crooked and perverse people.**
> **Philippians 2:15 NLT**

Holiness, innocence and purity are all concepts and commands we've discussed in previous sections. The warning here is that the people of this crooked world are ever watching and waiting for a Christian to slip up.

Why do they do this? Because perversity loves scandal.

There is nothing the enemy enjoys more than when we impede or block or short-circuit the light that we are called to shine. There is a wise proverb that says, "Don't give people an excuse to believe the worst about you."

Again, we are encouraged by the Apostle Paul to keep grace and truth in balance as we go about our daily lives and reach out for God's dream for us in this world:

> **For you were once darkness, but** now you are light **in the Lord.** Walk as children of light, **for the** fruit of the light **consists in all goodness, righteousness, and truth.**
>
> **Test and prove what pleases the Lord...**
>
> **But** everything exposed by the light becomes visible, **for** everything that is illuminated becomes a light **itself.**
> **Ephesians 5:8-10, 13 BSB**

Darkness use to be in our DNA, but not anymore. "Thy Word is a lamp unto my feet and a light unto my path." (See Psalms 119:105.) So your journey should be in step with the light of Scripture serving as your guide.

To prove whether something will bring value in our lives, we are to take the measuring stick of the Bible and lay it alongside to test how it measures up.

When your life is shining in the light of the Holy Spirit, you're not afraid of being exposed, because all is already visible. There is no shame for those who live purely for God's pleasure.

As we close this chapter, perhaps the line in verse 13 (above) is the most provocative of all:

"Everything that is illuminated becomes a light itself."

For a moment, let yourself be pulled into the gravity of such a statement! What all could this possibly mean? Thoughts shift to where it says, "the riches of the glory of this mystery, which is Christ in you, the hope of glory." (See Colossians 1:27.)

The full expression of Christ's light that we carry is certainly a mystery with at least two certainties:

One, we often live far below the capabilities of the gift of the Holy Spirit within us.

Two, we must shine our lights in this dark and despairing world.

△△△

1. My TAKE AWAY from this chapter is...

2. This chapter makes me GRATEFUL because...

3. I will TAKE ACTION for this by...

4.3 | PRAY FOR WORKERS

When He saw the crowds, He had compassion for them, because they were harassed and helpless, like sheep without a shepherd.

Then He said to his disciples, "The harvest is plentiful, but the laborers are few; therefore pray earnestly to the Lord of the harvest to send out laborers **into His harvest."**
Matthew 9:36-38 ESV

Which do you feel best describes your approach to life:

Control-minded *or* growth-minded?

Status quo *or* ongoing development?

Welcoming others in *or* putting up barriers against?

Your responses determine how effective you are in helping build God's Kingdom. Never forget that this is your number one priority as a Christ-follower.

Above, Jesus presents two profound word pictures to get our hearts and heads in the right place:

First, He models a shepherd's heart for those who are broken, struggling and weak. Rather than a harsh bully who pushes people into doing our bidding, we are called to be loving guides who attract and lead people towards the hope that can only be found in Christ.

Second, Jesus illuminates our awareness to see that the opportunity for the gospel is always ripe for harvest. Sometimes we can feel alone in our walk with God or like we're the only ones who care. That's an arrogantly religious mindset to have! Often, when we hit a plateau in our journey like this, it's because we're entering a new season where we are called to start sowing into others rather than merely being sowed into.

Authentic closeness to God equates to an ever growing passion for others.

Luke's account builds on this notion:

> **And He was saying to them, "The harvest is plentiful, but the laborers are few; therefore** plead with the Lord of the harvest to send out laborers **into His harvest.**
>
> **Go; behold, I am sending you out like lambs in the midst of wolves."**
> **Luke 10:2-3 NASB**

Jesus was effectively coaching his disciples to get their minds on the big picture. Urging them to "plead" for more harvesters, in addition to being ready to mentor the next generation when they reveal themselves.

Recognize that Jesus is not telling His disciples that He's sending them out in the "land of lollipops and gumdrops," but rather that He's sending them out as "lambs in the midst of wolves." Anyone who's ever been bold in their faith knows what it's like to have the world threaten to silence their voice.

Adding to the compounding effect, there are not only the wolves who are obviously out to get us, but also the "wolves in sheep's clothing." One could easily begin to feel quite intimidated. There are those who want to silence us, and those who want to pose as a part of Christ's Body, but are doing so out of deceitful, selfish motives.

Jesus shares His cosmic plan for ultimately removing the "weeds":

> **...while you are pulling the weeds, you may uproot the wheat with them.**
>
> **Let both grow together until the harvest. At that time I will tell the harvesters: "First collect the weeds and tie them in bundles to be burned; then gather the wheat and bring it into my barn."**
> **Matthew 13:29-30 NIV**

God knows exactly whose hearts fully belong to Him, and who the imposters are. He promises ultimate judgment on those who mean His Kingdom harm. He even gives an extra level of warning to those who would become stumbling blocks or whose hidden agenda is to manipulate His people. (See Luke 17:1-2.)

Oh, but what a promise to those who are the true workers and to those who pray for and mentor other harvesters!

> **...wake up and look around. The fields are already ripe for harvest.**
>
> **The harvesters are paid good wages, and the fruit they harvest is people brought to eternal life. What joy awaits both the planter and the harvester alike!**
>
> **I sent you to harvest where you didn't plant; others had already done the work, and now you will get to gather the harvest.**

Jesus must have had Solomon's proverb in mind, "The fruit of the righteous is a tree of life, and he who wins souls is wise." (See Proverbs 11:30.)

There is no greater joy experienced or no greater blessing received than to harvest (or win) a soul to salvation in Christ! We've learned already that "the wages of sin is death." By contrast, we now also understand that the wages of redemption is blissful life everlasting. Not only yours, but also those of whom you've helped welcome into the Kingdom.

Standing on the shoulders of giants in the faith that have preceded us, we get to reap where they planted and watered. And, following the pattern, we are instructed to plant and water for those in our time, so that the next generation will have a harvest.

Can you imagine what that celebration will look like in Heaven, when each generation of God's people will get to witness the big, final picture of eternity?

ΔΔΔ

1. My TAKE AWAY from this chapter is...

2. This chapter makes me GRATEFUL because...

3. I will TAKE ACTION for this by...

4.4 | LET THE HOLY SPIRIT TEACH YOU

Now when they bring you to the synagogues and magistrates and authorities, do not worry about how or what you should answer, or what you should say.

For the Holy Spirit will teach you in that very hour what you ought to say.
Luke 12:11-12 NKJV

How very peculiar a statement! Even more bizarre, this teaching immediately follows Christ's warning about blaspheming the Holy Spirit. (See verses 8-10.)

Remember the Holy Spirit had not yet been accessible to man in the way Jesus was describing it soon would be. The significance of all this could not be overstated. Jesus was predicting literal life or death situations and then instructing his disciples in how to approach them.

Being brought before religious and political leaders who could determine your very life's fate, one might imagine that it would be better to be prepared rather than just "winging it." But is that, in fact, what Jesus is commanding those advocating on His behalf? We think not.

First, the command seems to be strategically specific in the sense that we are to not "worry," as opposed to anything else. (More on the subject of worry in a moment.)

Second, the Holy Spirit is the Wonderful Counselor, as well as the ultimate Advocate. We are indeed called to preparation for moments of duress like these, though in a very strange, yet beautiful way. Jesus explains this in John's gospel:

> **There is so much more I want to tell you, but you can't bear it now.**
>
> When the Spirit of truth comes, He will guide you into all truth. **He will not speak on His own but will tell you what He has heard...**
>
> He will bring Me glory by telling you **whatever He receives from Me.**
> John 16:12-14 NLT

We are all expected to "study to show ourselves approved." (See 2 Timothy 2:15.) Likewise, we are called into deep fellowship with Christ through means of the Holy Spirit. Our preparedness for success in such moments of opposition relies completely on His help. But why?

Because the Holy Spirit reveals, exposes and unlocks the secret things inside the heart. It does so in a way that far surpasses anything that could be presented by mere human argumentation.

However, there are prerequisites to this type of access. Heartfelt worship, faith-filled prayer and passionate study of God's Word all help develop your "ear to hear" from God. The Holy Spirit provides a language of ascent for Christ's followers that cannot be derived by mere human means alone. He teaches the secret things of God to those who are hungry for more.

For balance sake, also note that fellowship with the Holy Spirit isn't cooky or spooky. When it's truly from God, it is spot on and undeniable. Clear and cutting right to the heart of the matter. Pointed, yet expansive enough to reach every nation, tribe and tongue. As we learn next from Mark's Gospel:

> **You will stand before governors and kings for My sake, as a testimony to them.**
>
> **And the gospel must first be preached to all the nations.**
>
> **...do not worry beforehand about what you are to say, but** say whatever is given you at that time; **for you are not the ones speaking, but** it is the Holy Spirit.
> **Mark 13:9-11 NASB**

So back to the matter of *worry.*

Just as the Holy Spirit reveals, He also empowers. We are not to worry as though we were children fearful about what to tell our parents when we've done something wrong.

When we consistently profess and live out our faith, our submitted lifestyles and words become increasingly interwoven with the Holy Spirit. Thus, giving greater weight (and confidence) to what we say in an otherwise tense moment. It is to boldness—mind you, not rudeness—that we are called.

Thank God! There will be a day when all will not need to be taught because all will know. The prophet Jeremiah shares this promise from God:

> **"No longer will each man teach his neighbor or his brother, saying, 'Know the LORD,'** because they will all know Me, **from the least of them to the greatest," declares the LORD. "For I will forgive**

their iniquities and will remember their sins no more."
Jeremiah 31:34 BSB

The Holy Spirit already teaches outside the boundaries of what the human mind can comprehend alone. Can you imagine what it will be like when all our human restraints are broken and we can know God for who He is?

What a wonderful day that will be!

Get as close as you will and as deep as you will and God will take you deeper still. Let the Holy Spirit teach you what to say and how to live. Then, you will lead a remarkable life! One that you'll never regret. One that brings true joy.

△△△

1. My TAKE AWAY from this chapter is...

2. This chapter makes me GRATEFUL because...

3. I will TAKE ACTION for this by...

4.5 | DEMONSTRATE GOD'S POWER

When He had called His twelve disciples to Him, He gave them power...

And as you go, preach, **saying, "The Kingdom of Heaven is at hand.**

Heal **the sick,** cleanse **the lepers,** raise **the dead,** cast out **demons. Freely you have received, freely give."**

Matthew 10:1, 7-8 NKJV

Before organizations release their final product or service, they usually prep their teams for what's referred to as a "soft launch." This accomplishes a number of things prior to going fully public. One of these being that it exposes any glitches or adjustments that need to be made so the team can more accurately represent the intended vision and mission.

At the risk of this illustration sounding too business-oriented, we enter a very similar type of scene with Jesus preparing his team for their "test run."

These same men would soon become the first chief executives and board of directors for Christ's Church. Everybody starts somewhere and Jesus was building something that would change everything about man's connection to God! Jesus' "product" was Himself and the services rendered would be nothing less than man's very salvation, as well as access to the Holy Spirit's power.

We were never meant to attempt life on our power alone, for we ultimately have none. Paul explains:

For I resolved to know nothing... except Jesus Christ and Him crucified.

I came to you in weakness with great fear and trembling.

My message and my preaching were not with wise and persuasive words, but with a demonstration of the Spirit's power, so that your faith might not rest on human wisdom, but on God's power.
1 Corinthians 2:2-5 NIV

With incredible insight, Paul's statement above faithfully manages the tension between confidence and humility. Make no mistakes, the man was a genius and formally trained at the highest levels available in Jewish education. Yet, he humbly realizes that what he contributed, in and of himself, was nothing in comparison to the demonstration of the Spirit's power.

These demonstrations of power were the certificate of authenticity that proved an apostle's alignment with God's Word and the gospel of Jesus Christ.

In a second letter to the church at Corinth, Paul describes the power of the Holy Spirit coming to his aid in the darkest of times. We are inspired to never take our eyes off the prize, no matter what comes our way:

But as servants of God we commend ourselves in every way: by great endurance, in afflictions, hardships, calamities, beatings, imprisonments,

riots, labors, sleepless nights, hunger;

by purity, knowledge, patience, kindness, the Holy Spirit, genuine love; by truthful speech, and the power of God; with the weapons of righteousness for the right hand and for the left;

2 Corinthians 6:4-7 ESV

The coupling of truthful speech, as well as the power of God, is a combination that sends all of Hell begging for mercy. Exercising our righteousness in Christ is a formidable weapon against any weapon formed against us.

So how do we exercise this gift? We speak God's Word.

We boldly agree with what God has already said in the areas of healing, blessing, miracles, discernment and warnings. It's up to God to perform His work when matched with His Word. Pray for wisdom, timing and alignment. Speak faithfully to situations with what God has already said.

The believer can endure anything that life throws at him or her. We are given all that we could ever need in Him:

For His divine power has granted to us everything pertaining to life and godliness, through the true knowledge of Him who called us by His own glory and excellence.

Through these He has granted to us His precious and magnificent promises, so that by them you may become partakers of the divine nature, having escaped the corruption that is in the world...

2 Peter 1:3-4 NASB

God has provided the power source of His Holy Spirit to all of humankind. Access is readily available to all who truly desire to know Him.

Jesus not only provides the means of escape, but also extends the coveted invitation to "partake in His divine nature." This world (and even sometimes, we Christians) are willing to settle for far less by "having a form of godliness but denying the power thereof." (See 2 Timothy 3:5.)

One sober reminder is also fitting here: Lucifer (Satan) got kicked out of Heaven because of the pride he placed in his God-given power rather than the God who gave it.

Understand that these demonstrations of power are meant to point people to worship God alone. It is a precious and holy gift. Treat it as such. Demonstrate His power by speaking His Word, then give God the glory when all are amazed at the results.

△△△

1. My TAKE AWAY from this chapter is...

2. This chapter makes me GRATEFUL because...

3. I will TAKE ACTION for this by...

4.6 | FREELY GIVE

And as you go, preach, saying, "The Kingdom of Heaven is at hand."

Heal the sick, cleanse the lepers, raise the dead, cast out demons. Freely you have received, freely give.

Matthew 10:7-8 NKJV

In our last chapter, we discussed this passage with our focus on "demonstrating God's power." Now, we'll double down on this directive with a special emphasis on what it means to "freely give" and how we can go about it. Giving is a central theme running throughout all of Scripture.

God is the ultimate gift giver. He gave us His one and only Son. Then He also gave us His Holy Spirit. And it's through this same Spirit that we are given gifts that we can, in turn, give as our gifts to this world.

Ephesians 2:10 teaches us four pithy principles about freely giving what you have received:

First, you are a gift.

Second, you are gifted.

Third, you are given opportunities to freely use your gifting.

Fourth, you walk in your purpose when you operate through your gifting.

Sadly, and for whatever reason, few are often committed to a lifestyle of freely giving. Maybe it's the fear of inadequacy or intimidation. Perhaps it's just simple, close-fisted greed. As Christ-followers, we must battle against these fleshly tendencies. We must learn the power of generosity set within the gospel, alongside our God-given gifting. Proverbs tells us:

> One person gives freely, yet gains more; **another withholds what is right, only to become poor.**
> **Proverbs 11:24 HCSB**

Again, whatever it may be that tempts you to hold back your gifting, will inevitably hold back your entire life.

Experiencing genuine fulfillment is the harvest of good deeds sown from generous seeds. When we hold back from freely giving, we only cheat ourselves out of God's abundant grace and favor.

It's been said, "God has called us to be funnels of His blessing and not merely buckets." Meaning that whatever God is pouring *into* us was also meant to be poured *through* us.

Joyful generosity is the hallmark of the believer. Listen to this passage:

> **You shall** give to him freely, **and your heart shall not be grudging when you give to him, because for this the LORD your God will bless you in all your work and in all that you undertake.**
> **Deuteronomy 15:10 ESV**

The gap between what you have now and what you will have in the future is bridged by what you are willing to give of yourself in the meantime.

And just as important is the attitude fueling your giving. What do we mean by this? Good question.

Similar to the above passage from Deuteronomy, the Apostle Paul uses a similar expression of being a "cheerful giver." (See 2 Corinthians 9:7.)

Have you ever seen someone give, yet complain about it the entire time? It's not pretty, it's petty. Definitely not the attitude nor the kind of gift that God will bless. Our time, our talent and our treasure is affected more by *how* we give, over and above *what* we give.

We properly reflect God's love to a lost and dying world when we take on the same mindset as Christ. This is fundamentally important to understand when it comes to generosity. As always, Jesus leads by example:

> ...(Jesus) said to me, "It is done! I am the Alpha and the Omega, the beginning and the end. I will freely give to the thirsty from the spring of the water of life.
>
> The one who conquers will inherit these things, and I will be His God, and he will be My son."
>
> **Revelation 21:6-7 CSB**

We would do well to ponder more often and more deeply how much God wants to freely give of Himself to us, His children.

Blessings being withheld is more likely a result of our own unpreparedness to receive them. He is always looking for empty vessels to pour into in such a way that it would be "pressed down, shaken, and running over" in our lives. (See Luke 6:38.)

God wants to freely disperse life, victory and heirship to those who follow Him. All it takes is for us to have the same willingness. To be funnels of His blessing and favor. Freely giving, because we've freely received.

$$\triangle \triangle \triangle$$

1. My TAKE AWAY from this chapter is...

2. This chapter makes me GRATEFUL because...

3. I will TAKE ACTION for this by...

4.7 | DON'T FEAR

I tell you, my friends, do not fear those who kill the body, and after that have nothing more that they can do.

But I will warn you whom to fear: fear Him who, after He has killed, has authority to cast into hell. Yes, I tell you, fear Him!

Luke 12:4-5 ESV

Sometimes it takes radical bravery to live the fullest expression of what it means to be a child of God.

It grieves the Holy Spirit when we cower away from opportunities to represent Him faithfully because of the fear of other people. Whether the situation manifests itself among family, friends or foes, we are to stand firm nonetheless. In a generation wrestling with attacks on the very nature of identity, we as Christ-followers find our surest foundation in identifying with Him.

We have joined ourselves with The King of Kings. This should give us great courage.

In the passage above, Jesus lays out a weighty comparison that seems unbearably heavy. This hard truth seems to be lost on many of us today and it's no wonder. It's not a fun one to talk about. However difficult it may seem, Jesus gives solid reasoning behind His teaching by abruptly shifting the object of our fear. He asks us:

"Who should you be more afraid of dishonoring, disobeying or distancing yourself from—Man or God?"

Have you ever thought about that? Take a minute to compare the consequences of each. While it should be a no brainer, it somehow still proves to be a more difficult decision than it should be. Why is this?

Our daily interactions tend to expose the fact that our awareness tends toward the presence of other humans rather than the Presence of God.

To be sure, there is a lot to say about what "fearing God" actually means. (We'll address this point at the close of our chapter, but Jesus' own comparison in Luke 12 seems to paint a deeply disturbing picture indeed!)

First, let's discuss walking in confidence rather than in the fear of man. Isaiah prophesies:

> **So do not fear, for I am with you; do not be dismayed, for I am your God. I will strengthen you and help you; I will uphold you with my righteous right hand.**
>
> **All who rage against you will surely be ashamed and disgraced;**
> **Isaiah 41:10-11 NIV**

Worthy admiration awaits a Christian who doesn't bail, balk or buckle in the face of opposition.

Being truly awe-inspiring to witness, there is something supernatural (no surprise) about someone who unquestionably trusts God's provision and protection. Someone who does so, even in the midst of the most terrible spiritual battles. For those so bold, God promises an indestructible reward as well as a powerful life's legacy.

The Apostle Peter further arouses our courage:

Who is there to harm you if you prove zealous for what is good?

But even if you should suffer for the sake of righteousness, you are blessed. And do not fear their intimidation **and do not be in dread...**

1 Peter 3:13-14 NASB

Peter brilliantly makes the case for exercising fearlessness in doing what is good and right. Most people appreciate seeing a good thing done, whether they believe in a God or not. However, we understand it may not always feel that way. Maybe it's because we live among a generation that "calls evil good and good evil." (See Isaiah 5:20.)

Peter anticipates that possibility as well and is telling us emphatically: "So what! Be godly at all costs and don't be intimidated by anyone when it comes to living the Christian life!"

As we close this chapter, let's finally address what is meant by the "fear of God" when contrasted with the "fear of man." In our beginning passage, we are taught that we should weigh these two in the balance.

So, who controls where you will spend eternity? God or man? Make no mistake, until you fully come to grips with the propensity for God's wrath, you'll likely never fully comprehend the depth of His mercy and love. Elsewhere we discover that "The fear of the Lord is the beginning of wisdom." (See Proverbs 9:10.)

Even a small child can imagine a potential punishment ahead of time and then make the right choice in the end. How much more should a legitimate fear of eternal consequence motivate a similar course correction for us?

Though, remember that a "healthy fear" represents only the "beginning of wisdom." Spiritual maturity is achieved when we do what's right for its own sake. Stemming from a place of authentic love, rather than fear:

> There is no fear in love (dread does not exist). But perfect (complete, full-grown) love drives out fear, because fear involves (the expectation of divine) punishment, so the one who is afraid (of God's judgment) is not perfected in love (has not grown into a sufficient understanding of God's love).
>
> We love, because He first loved us.
> 1 John 4:18-19 AMP

Genuine Christ-like love, as we've learned in previous chapters, brings ultimate fulfillment.

We've now also learned that it has the ability to eradicate any fears that would otherwise attempt to cripple us. Our Heavenly Father's will is not to keep us under His thumb, but rather to reveal His very heart. He loved us first.

Those in Christ have neither need nor reason to fear God's wrath.

Perfect love casts out all fear.

△△△

1. My TAKE AWAY from this chapter is...

2. This chapter makes me GRATEFUL because...

3. I will TAKE ACTION for this by...

4.8 | WAKE UP!

...I know your deeds; you have a reputation of being alive, but you are dead.

Wake up! Strengthen what remains and is about to die, for I have found your deeds unfinished in the sight of my God.
Revelation 3:1-2 NIV

Out of the many commands of Christ that we've examined thus far, this certainly is one of the most sobering.

So, what can we learn from this rebuke that is meant to keep us awakened and aware of God's will for our lives?

The church at Sardis (the ones being addressed in this letter) apparently had a healthy reputation among other churches at the time. That being said, we still see Christ coaxing them out of a spiritual slumber of sorts.

There is a season where, if not careful, an individual believer or even a group of believers (i.e. a church) can become complacent and begin to coast in their discipleship. In truth, our journey is not finished until we pass out of this life and into the next. It can become so easy to think that we have arrived and that there's no further development needed.

However, what is stagnant becomes complacent and what is complacent becomes arrogant. When we begin to feel a spiritual laziness like this, Christ calls on us to "wake up and finish the work!"

Jesus continues this thread of thought in the next verse:

Remember, therefore, what you have received and heard; hold it fast, and repent. But if you do not wake up, I will come like a thief, **and you will not know at what time I will come to you.**

Revelation 3:3 NIV

There are many full-circle moments in the life of the believer. A positive example of this would be the experience of helping others through a season of life in which we ourselves have succeeded. Nothing is more rewarding than becoming the "Paul" to someone else's "Timothy."

By contrast, when we have to relearn a forgotten lesson, we run the risk of losing face and grieving the Holy Spirit. Additionally, when we're not constantly practicing our discipleship, we sadly miss out on the joy of helping others while also further engraining the practice into the fabric our own lives.

God's grace and mercy is sufficient for most missed opportunities, which is why repentance is so vital when we slip. However, for those who continue to abuse this principle, they may eventually find themselves lulled into such a sleep that they miss a significant Divine appointment. One that could have completely changed their life's trajectory for the better. Can you imagine the embarrassment?

Paul echos Christ's call to "wake up" the Ephesians:

Wake up, sleeper! **Arise from the dead, and the Messiah will shine on you.**

So, then, be careful how you live. Do not be unwise but wise, making the best use of your time because the times are evil.

Have you ever been suddenly awakened by a bright light shining down on your face?

This is precisely the illustration that Paul is drawing from to make his point. What happened when the light hit you? Did it energize you to begin your day? Did you try to cover your eyes and roll over and hit the snooze button? Now consider these same types of questions in the climate of your walk with God.

Does the Son's light energize you or do you find yourself, as of late, resisting it more often? If it's the latter, it's time to wake up!

Paul further cautions us to be careful of how we live out our lives. Why? Because, as we've said in previous chapters, people are watching. We are to steward and align ourselves around God's highest and best use for us in His Kingdom. The pursuit of what this means for each of us individually is what makes living for God so exciting!

This closing passage becomes the war cry for all spiritual warriors. The Lord says through the prophet Joel:

> **Prepare for war!** Wake up the mighty men, **Let all the men of war draw near, Let them come up.**
>
> **Beat your plowshares into swords and your pruning hooks into spears; Let the weak say, "I am strong.**
> **"**
>
> **Joel 3:9-10 NKJV**

You can almost feel your chest bow up a little bit when you read this! What an incredible rally cry. We must never lose sight of the fact that we are equipped and expected to engage in spiritual warfare. Christ-followers have never been called to passivity or weakness.

Every time the church answers the cry to wake up: Individuals become more bold, families become restored, communities become safer and even nations become beneficiaries of the grace and goodness of God.

There are times for building with tools, just as there are times for defending those same buildings with weapons. We understand that our spiritual weapons are different however. "We are human, but we don't wage war as humans do. We use God's mighty weapons, not worldly weapons, to knock down the strongholds of human reasoning and to destroy false arguments." (See 2 Corinthians 10:3-4.)

So, wake up! Keep fighting the good fight.

ΔΔΔ

1. My TAKE AWAY from this chapter is...

2. This chapter makes me GRATEFUL because...

3. I will TAKE ACTION for this by...

4.9 | HOLD ON TO WHAT YOU HAVE

I am coming soon. Hold on to what you have, **so that no one will take your crown.**
Revelation 3:11 NIV

So far, as you've read and put into practice the things in this book, you've undoubtedly gained much ground in your walk with God. Congratulations!

Now, "hold on to what you have!"

This is what we hear Jesus telling the church at Philadelphia. A command that still rings true for us all today, in whichever church you find yourself a part.

We, like them, are also pulled into the gravity of Christ's imminent return. God is still weaving His perfect will into the tapestry and the history of humanity. It is notable that, in our last chapter as well as this one, Christ is issuing these warnings to established churches and individuals alike.

Practically speaking, how can one hold on to what they have if they don't already have it?

This is a crucial concept to nail down. Why? Because the goal of this warning is not to invoke a fear of losing one's salvation, but rather the loss of additional heavenly reward. Similar to Jesus' teaching on the parable of the talents, Christ is wanting to add to our eternal experience through rewards and blessings that will last forever. The crown mentioned in the verse above symbolizes the revelation that those who are faithful will indeed rule with Christ. (See 1 Corinthians 6:1-3.)

Unlike our salvation, this "crown" is not guaranteed. But what could possibly rob us of such a reward?

Ironically and sadly enough, only we ourselves can cause this. When we slide back into the sinful lifestyles we've renounced, we run a high risk of losing out on God's best for us. Read what Jesus warns another church (Thyatira) about chasing after sinful things:

> **I have this against you: You tolerate that woman Jezebel... By her teaching she misleads my servants into sexual immorality and the eating of food sacrificed to idols.**
>
> **...do not hold to her teaching and... Satan's so-called deep secrets,**
> **Revelation 2:20, 24 NIV**

What we tolerate in our lives may perhaps be, to some extent, overlooked as a result of God's mercy as well. Why chance it though? It is more likely we'll end up cheating ourselves out of the more abundant life of which we are in pursuit. In our present and broken state, we never completely lose our taste for temptation. There exists a lure that is meant to bait each one of us. The forces of evil would love nothing more than to get its hooks into us and trap us.

Don't be seduced by the enemy of your soul!

Let's also be clear that "holding on to what you have" isn't permission to stop at a point in your walk with God. We are called to always be conquering new territory for Christ until He comes. Jesus continues in His letter:

Just hold on to what you have **until I come.**

To the person who conquers and continues to do what I've commanded to the end, I will give authority over the nations.
Revelation 2:25-26 ISV

So we see that it's clearly not okay to suddenly (or even slowly) become passive in our faith, merely holding on to yesterday's victories. Quite the contrary, and with our grip firmly on one rung, we are to use that momentum to propel ourselves to the next.

We are called to be conquerors. But just how do we do this?

Continue to be "light" and "salt" everywhere you go. Continue to pair God's grace and truth in your dealings with others. Continue to seek opportunity to present the gospel, in word and in deed.

Be consistent in these practices and you will begin to notice these full circle moments. Moments where you are no longer only the hearer, but now the doer as well as the deliverer of God's Word and His love.

So, what exactly are we to "hold on to" then? Paul teaches these inarguable and indisputable truths. We are to never compromise these:

...hold fast to the word I preached to you—**unless you believed in vain.**

For I delivered to you as of first importance what I also received: **that Christ died for our sins in accordance with the Scriptures, that He was buried, that He was raised on the third day in**

accordance with the Scriptures,

and that He appeared... appeared... appeared... appeared...

1 Corinthians 15:2-8 ESV

The expression "hold fast" carries with it the image of a vice-like grip onto something. "Holding on for dear life," as they say. Paul is not overstating how inflexible the tenets of the death, burial and resurrection of Jesus Christ actually are. It is central and foundational to everything else. He knew that we must hold fast to this truth, or else half-truths and heresy would begin to creep their way into our minds and hearts.

Paul points to a plethora of Messianic prophecy, in conjunction with a long list of first-hand, eye-witness testimony to make his case regarding Christ's death, burial and resurrection.

We understand that in the Mosaic law, proof was established by at least two and preferably three witnesses. Paul provides four incontrovertible testimonies of Christ's appearances after His death. The implications to which have created volumes of masterful works over many a century.

Hold on to all that you have learned so far!

ΔΔΔ

1. My TAKE AWAY from this chapter is...

2. This chapter makes me GRATEFUL because...

3. I will TAKE ACTION for this by...

4.10 | DO THE WORKS YOU DID AT FIRST

Remember the heights from which you have fallen, and repent (change your inner self—your old way of thinking, your sinful behavior—seek God's will) and do the works you did at first (when you first knew Me); otherwise, I will visit you and remove your lampstand (the church, its impact) from its place—unless you repent.

Revelation 2:5 AMP

These last few chapters may seem heavy-handed when compared to the others. Maybe you're even reading this and thinking, "I'm really trying here. What's with the threats all of a sudden?"

Be patient. Be encouraged. Keep reading and give careful attention. Discover to whom this warning is intended.

You see, much like the church at Ephesus (the original recipients of this letter), this teaching isn't for the moments when you're faithfully walking in obedience. It's for the seasons when you're not. Your faithfulness to the process is proof that it does indeed matter to you. We celebrate your progress!

This is a call to those seasons of our lives when honest, humble reflection reveals that we've gotten off track in our walk with God. We lose our ability for eternal impact when our relationship with God devolves into nothing more than empty religion.

The collective body of Christ serve as His only ambassadors to a lost and dying world. God has no Plan B in mind to reach the lost other than through His Church. The stakes couldn't be higher. Jesus reminds us to get back on center with the mission.

Spectacularly as always, Jesus leads by example. Look at His attitude and actions, always laser-focused the mission:

> **I must** work the works of Him who sent Me **while it is day; the night is coming when no one can work.**
>
> **As long as I am in the world, I am the light of the world.**
> **John 9:4-5 NKJV**

Astonishingly, He invites us to partner with Him in His mission. His very own life modeled His preaching. Essentially saying, "While I have breath in this body, I will not stop being and bringing the light of God's truth and love to this world!"

While we still have time—however much time that may be for each of us—keep doing the work!

So, just what is "the work" exactly? Very simple. Point people to Jesus. He takes care of the rest:

> **Believe Me when I say that I am in the Father and the Father is in Me; or at least** believe on the evidence of the works **themselves.**
>
> **Very truly I tell you,** whoever believes in Me will do the works I have been doing, **and they** will do even greater things **than these, because I am going to the Father.**
> **John 14:11-12 NIV**

We make note of at least a couple of ideas in play with this passage. All of them have to do with how "the works" actually works.

First, it is the finished work of Jesus' death, burial and resurrection that brings us salvation.

Next, the same Holy Spirit that fueled the works, ministry and miracles throughout Jesus' life is the same spirit that fuels our ability to do great and mighty works as well. (As we believe more deeply and faithfully in Him, we are given access to do miraculous things.)

Most of us are guilty of thinking too small, when in fact, we are called to "do greater things."

Capture the powerful significance of this passage we're exploring. This is part of our inheritance as a believer! God wants so passionately to work through our lives in powerful ways. Why? Again, to confirm Himself and His Word and His Truth through us.

He didn't just send the Holy Spirit to make us play nice, He did so to equip and empower us to be dangerous to all of Hell!

Maybe this is news to you or maybe you just needed the reminder. We've already talked about casting aside your fear. You're nearing the finish line of this book. Let the words of King David electrify your resolve to do the work:

> **Then David continued, "Be strong and courageous, and do the work. Don't be afraid or discouraged, for the LORD God, my God, is with you. He will not fail you or forsake you. He will see to it that all the work related to the Temple of the LORD is finished correctly."**
>
> **1 Chronicles 28:20 NLT**

There you have it: The ongoing work of your personal sanctification, plus the work of spreading the gospel proves to be an exhilarating ride.

Cast aside your fears and doubts. Don't compare yourself to others or worry about anyone else around you. Rest when you must, then get back up. Pull from the reservoir of God's strength. Encourage yourself in the Lord. Trust that He'll be with you in the darkest of moments. Seek the work that God has specifically called you to in His Kingdom.

Give it your best. That's all He expects.

△△△

1. My TAKE AWAY from this chapter is...

2. This chapter makes me GRATEFUL because...

3. I will TAKE ACTION for this by...

4.11 | FEED MY SHEEP

Jesus asked Simon Peter, "Simon son of John, do you love Me more than these?"

"Yes, Lord," Peter replied, "you know I love you."

He (Jesus) said to him, "Then feed My lambs,"

..."Then take care of My sheep,"

..."Then feed My sheep."
John 21:15-17 NLT

One thing is for absolute certain: The heart and the will of God is profoundly simple and incredibly consistent throughout the entirety of Scripture.

We witness this being played out in a very visceral and personal appeal from Jesus to Peter. The two greatest commandments, "Love God and love people," are brought back into unmistakable focus.

The scene painted above crescendos into Jesus guiding Peter through the exercise of repenting for his three-fold denial, occurring only days earlier. Regardless of what it might cost him from now on, Peter is reclaiming and recommitting his fidelity to his Rabbi and Savior. Peter's scope is then extended beyond their personal relationship as he begins to recognize that it's not merely about just himself anymore. He and his fellow disciples are about to become "the Apostles." They are about to spend the rest of their lives feeding others, as they have been fed.

Jesus presents the if/then proposition of our love for Him. We prove we love Him by caring for others on Christ's behalf. As we reach a certain stage in our faith, this expectation could not be more revelatory (or more rewarding.)

God has no toleration whatsoever for those whose focus and faith is self-centered. Listen to God's words through the prophet Ezekiel in the Old Testament:

My shepherds have not searched for My sheep, but the shepherds have fed themselves, and have not fed My sheep, **therefore, you shepherds, hear the word of the LORD:**

"Behold, I am against the shepherds, and I will require My sheep at their hand and put a stop to their feeding the sheep.**"**
Ezekiel 34:8-10 ESV

To be fair, those that are relatively new to faith, your priority is solely to first develop yourself as a disciple. That's why we spent a lot of time developing these concepts in the first two sections of this book. As your understanding continues to grow however, you should begin experiencing a shift more rich in its *outward* expression rather than it being solely *inward.*

That being said, never forget the *upward* expression of your faith. This is the "sure and steadfast anchor of your soul."

We all have some degree of influence. Most usually though, we hear the term "shepherd" in the Bible and think only of pastors or priests. This is of course accurate, but not limited to these offices alone. We are all responsible for expanding God's Kingdom and our influence in bringing people into it. For you, this may mean your family, your friends, or someone you haven't even met yet.

You may be asking by now, "How (or with what) exactly are we supposed to be feeding God's sheep?" The prophet Jeremiah helps us better understand this:

> **"And I will give you** shepherds according to My heart, who will feed you **with knowledge and understanding.**
>
> **Then it shall come to pass, when you are multiplied and increased in the land in those days," says the Lord.**
>
> **Jeremiah 3:15-16 NKJV**

So the shepherd is to be a ready supply of godly experience, knowledge and understanding to those who are hungry for God's Word. A true shepherd's heart is to be a heaven-sent haven to others. We are motivated by the multiplying of Christ's followers and the increase of God's Kingdom. Be always on the lookout for how you can leverage any given moment for God's glory.

Pulling on this thread a little more, what exactly is the heart of the ultimate Shepherd Himself? Isaiah reveals:

> **Yes, the Sovereign LORD is coming in power. He will rule with a powerful arm. See, He brings His reward with Him as He comes.**
>
> He will feed His flock like a shepherd. **He will carry the lambs in His arms, holding them close to His heart. He will gently lead the mother sheep with their young.**
>
> **Isaiah 40:10-11 NLT**

Look to Christ's example as you care for and feed His sheep.

Above, we read a messianic prophecy of exactly how Jesus would be coming soon to model this for us. It paints a beautiful picture of God's heart for the care of others.

Several redemptive attributes are brought to the surface by Isaiah. We see someone who exhibits authority and power, yet pairs it with tenderness. Someone with an ever-observant eye, who rewards faithfulness and loyalty. Still yet, someone who knows how to carry those that are weak, as well as gently lead those who may be timid or easily frightened.

As you continue to grow in your ambassadorship, you will notice all kinds of people that you will attract. The most positive possibility being those that are genuinely hungry to hear about your experience, so they can enter a relationship with God for themselves. Keep your eyes open for these moments and opportunities.

Don't feel the pressure to be something you're not. Simply seek to serve their need by feeding them with the nutrition of God's Word.

A shepherd's care is exhibited in meaningful prayer and the encouragement you share with others.

△△△

1. My TAKE AWAY from this chapter is...

2. This chapter makes me GRATEFUL because...

3. I will TAKE ACTION for this by...

4.12 | GO AND MAKE DISCIPLES

**Go therefore and make disciples of all the nations,
baptizing them in the Name of the Father and of
the Son and of the Holy Spirit, teaching them to
observe all things that I have commanded you;
and lo, I am with you always, even to the end of
the age. Amen.**
Matthew 28:19-20 NKJV

What an incredible journey we've been on together!

You began long ago by answering Jesus' initial challenge to simply, "Come and see." (See chapter 1.1.)

And as you've reached this final chapter, you've also arrived at a heart-thumping, full-circle, what-happens-next kind of moment!

The moment when Jesus now calls you to "Go and make disciples."

(You may be asking, "Sounds both scary and fun! What does that mean though?")

You've taken incredible steps of faith by reading and discussing this book. You've married each of these commands with some sort of actionable step on your part. Undoubtedly, you've also experienced the fusion of God's Word bringing new found clarity, passion, purpose and boldness into your life.

You've become a first-hand eyewitness of how Christ's mission was ultimately designed to make your "joy be made full."

Congratulations!

(You are probably saying to yourself, "You still haven't told me what 'Go and make disciples' means and how to do it!" We know, we're just so excited for you and proud of you leaning into this journey! Okay, here we go...)

As we explore this final command to "go and make disciples," one can almost feel the mantle being handed down from one generation of Christ-followers to the next. Referred to as "The Great Commission," this mantle now falls on you (and others like you) who represent the next generation of God's witnesses and ambassadors on this earth. His Church.

As an initial word of caution, remember to graciously and mercifully meet people where they are in their journey. Peter warns:

> **Why are you putting God to the test by placing a yoke on the neck of the disciples that neither our fathers nor we have been able to bear?**
>
> **But we believe that we will be saved through the grace of the Lord Jesus, just as they will.**
> **Acts 15:10-11 ESV**

Take great care to never trivialize the point at which someone else may be in their faith journey when compared to your own. That would be self-righteous and arrogant. Remember that it was often the pompous religious leaders that irritated, angered and disappointed the very heart of God.

Jesus was gentle and patient with you. Likewise, be gentle and patient with others.

Remember, the Holy Spirit does the work of saving, not us. Our role is to attract, guide and connect the dots for someone else in a way that presents Christ as He was intended to be. There's an old line that says, "If they don't like you, they sure won't like your Jesus." How true that is!

So, the goal is to "win" people to faith in Christ.

> **They preached the gospel in that city and** won a large number of disciples. **Then they returned...** strengthening the disciples **and encouraging them to remain true to the faith.**
> **Acts 14:21-22 NIV**

Notice the formula in the verses above:

First, they faithfully preached the gospel message that won people over.

Next, they returned to previously reached areas where they had done the same thing.

Then they strengthened them, encouraged them and challenged them to stay true to God.

The Kingdom of God is foundational yet fluid, centralized yet always expanding. It was built on truths solid enough to stand on and at the same time flexible enough for imperfect beings—such as ourselves—to gain entrance.

Just what does this look like when lived out practically? Phenomenal question. Here's Isaiah to show us:

> The Lord GOD has given me the tongue of disciples, **So that I may know how to sustain the weary one with a word. He awakens me morning by morning,** He awakens my ear to listen as a disciple.
> **Isaiah 50:4 NASB**

And there it is: Learn to love to learn.

Even as you've reached the stage to begin discipling others, never stop following and learning for yourself. This is a magnificent, lifelong adventure.

Isaiah captures so well the heart of the disciple. That is, how to *be* one and how to *lead* one. We discover and are reminded that it starts every morning we are blessed to be alive. There's an implied expectancy as a disciple awakens: "What new thing will God teach me today? What new person will He bring into my life? What new adventure will God have for me?"

Mistakenly, people have often complained that God doesn't speak to them. Not true. As you've learned already, the Holy Spirit is always creatively speaking into the lives of those whose ears are longing for His voice. Reading the Bible trains your ear to hear what Jesus died to share with you.

God is searching and seeking for those who are willing to both listen and then act on His Word.

Lastly, we see Isaiah reference the "tongue" of the disciple. And to what end does he declare the value of such a thing?

To impress people? No.

To judge others harshly? Still, no.

He instructs that it is for the unequivocal reason that we might "know how to sustain the weary one with a word." May we all humbly walk in such a way.

May your words lift up the weary one.

And now also, may your life command the joy God intended for you. May your joy continue to be made full and may the overflow be poured into the next person who needs what you have discovered on this journey.

A *joy* that is both real and reachable as it is authentic and abundant.

A *joy* that only His commands... can command.

Now... Go and make disciples.

ΔΔΔ

1. My TAKE AWAY from this chapter is...

2. This chapter makes me GRATEFUL because...

3. I will TAKE ACTION for this by...

ACKNOWLEDGEMENTS

My deepest heartfelt appreciation to my parents. Pops, for waking me up early to memorize Scripture at a very young age. I will never forget those mornings you sacrificed an extra half hour to teach me how to pray and love God's Word. Mom, I shall never lose the steadfastness and kindness you both birthed in me, as well as modeled for me. Thanks for sheltering me in God's House.

Kirby, thank you for your wise counsel while putting the final touches on the paperback and hardcover versions of this book. You have long proved to be a cherished "little brother" in addition to a beloved "son in the faith."

Thank you to "Dr." Aaron, from whom I totally stole the famous acronym *HABU*. (Highest and best use.) This is one of my favorite filters and principles for assessing value. I applied it many times in the framework of this writing.

Overwhelming thank you to BibleHub.com for your phenomenal search engine and incredibly robust study tools. This project would have taken so much longer to complete without your labor of love in making the Bible more accessible to the world.

CONNECT WITH THE AUTHOR

(1) You Can Connect With Me Directly On Any Of These Social Platforms!

Instagram - @travismarshall4

Facebook - @travismarshall4

Twitter - @travismarshall4

YouTube - @thinkknowlivemedia

(2) Coming Soon!!! Get Ready To Amplify Your Joy Experience By Joining Our Discipleship Nanocourse And Community.

(3) We'll Work To Make Sure You're Aware Of Any New Products We're Creating Or Projects We're Up To!

Made in the USA
Middletown, DE
01 March 2023

25650924R00126